And
Baby
Makes
Four

And Baby Makes Four

Welcoming a Second Child into the Family

HILORY WAGNER

Quill

An Imprint of HarperCollinsPublishers

HarperCollins books may be purchased for educational, business, or sales promotional use. For information please write: Special Markets Department, HarperCollins Publishers Inc., 10 East 53rd Street, New York, NY 10022.

First Avon edition published 1998.

Reprinted in Quill 2003.

Library of Congress Cataloging-in-Publication Data
Wagner, Hilory.
  And baby makes four : welcoming a second child into the family /
    Hilory Wagner.
      p. cm.
Includes bibliographical references (p.203).
1. Second-born children. 2. Parenting. I. Title.
HQ777.22.W34 1998   98-6888
649'.1—dc21   CIP

ISBN 0-380-79505-1

  10 11 12 RRD 10 9 8

For Punchky and Pasha

Contents

PART III: YOUR NEW FAMILY

Acknowledgments

First, a hearty thank you to my agent, Jennie Dunham, for her efforts in finding this book a home and for listening to more stories about my children than any nonrelative should ever have to.

Many thanks, also, to Chris Condry, the editor of this book, for taking interest in this project, for her valuable, insightful comments and suggestions, and for understanding when kids and deadlines refused to share.

To those who answered my survey questions and shared intimate details about their lives, I hope that they know how much I appreciated the time they took with me—time that probably could have been better spent with the very kids we were discussing! I'm grateful for all they've shared about their families: the triumphs, the trials, the surprises, the rewards, the ups and downs of their relationships, and all I could ever want to know about their children's potty habits.

In particular, I would like to recognize the warm, candid voices of America Online's Moms Online community. Dozens of women from these forums enthusiastically contributed personal anecdotes for these pages in hopes of helping other mothers of two or more. I've thanked them before and I'd like to thank them again for all the time they took to share their stories.

Finally, this book—and its central subjects, Sara and Joshua—would not have been possible without Jesse. To my husband and best friend I offer boundless thanks for his encouragement, his constant support, and for creating with me a house filled with warmth, humor, and love.

Introduction

It's 5: 30 P.M. on a Tuesday evening.

I am in the kitchen with my two young children on an already dark and frigid February night, attempting to prepare a rather simple spaghetti dinner for our family. Four-month-old Joshua has begun his usual early evening fussing. He isn't hungry or wet or ready for a nap. He most definitely does not want to lie on his quilt under the baby gym, or sit in either of his bouncy seats. So now he's in his swing, which unfortunately seems to have lost all of its magical pacifying power.

"Do the other one," says Sara, two and a half, her voice wavering. She is seated at the island by request, as she wanted to watch me cook. I've heard that tone before. If I don't do something fast, it will quickly escalate to a full-blown whine.

"What other one? What do you mean?" I say. I have no clue what she's talking about.

"Do the other one! The other one!" she says loudly, desperately. I glance at her hands, at the box of spaghetti, at the dog, behind me. I don't even see the "first one," so I have no idea what the "other one" could be.

"*What?*" I shout.

"Ehhhh, ehhhh, ehhhh," Josh continues, a complaining,

pathetic groan that's just loud enough to be impossible to tune out. Each progressive "ehhhh" pulls my shoulders one notch higher and one notch closer together, so that if I don't stop him soon, my head will explode.

"Rowrff! Rowrff!" barks Cooper, our Cardigan Welsh corgi, who is panic-stricken with the thought that after six years and a few thousand bowls of dog food, this will be the night I forget to feed him his dinner. "Rowrff! Rowrff! Rowrff!" he shouts frantically. He is wasting away!

"Do the other one!"

"Ehhhh!"

Sploooosh! Sizzzzzz! (Sound of boiling water running over the sides of the pot and onto the hot burner.)

I shout at Sara to stand back, quickly turning down the heat on the stove as the water steams and then chars the cooktop. I am practically overcome with a feeling of helplessness, sadness, and frustration as my charges continue to bark, whine, and fuss. I choke back a sob.

As my sneaker slides suddenly on a slimy substance, the room seems to spin out of control. The truth seems evident. I am powerless. Who was I to think I could handle so many—okay, two—children in addition to the loudest, most insistent dog on the planet? The phone rings. My husband tells me he'll be at the office another half hour at least.

Sara scans the room for the most dangerous appliance in sight and moves toward it. Cooper picks up something from the floor that crunches but probably shouldn't. Josh demands to be removed from the horrible swinging apparatus, and I realize I don't have any bread to serve with dinner.

I scoop up Josh and maneuver his little legs into his Exersaucer, basically a walker without wheels, which will buy me a few minutes. Since he can't hold toys very well, I sort of pile them in front of his hands, which serves more to hold him up than to amuse him. The drone continues. I consider joining the Federal Witness Protection Program.

Cooper gets his bowl of food, which, of course, takes

him completely by surprise. I return to the pot of pasta in defeat.

Suddenly, without my prompting, Sara moves toward the baby and picks up Sir Squeak-a-lot, a fuzzy, developmentally correct stuffed animal for which Josh has a particular affection. She squeezes it directly into his face a few times and giggles. Josh quiets, looking intently at the bear, then breaks into a broad, toothless grin. Sara smiles, then squeaks the bear again. Josh coos and squeals for all the world to hear. The dog, on the other hand, is silent. Sara beams at me and giggles again.

The sweetness has caught me off guard. I watch my children's smiles meet and I feel my heart, which had been racing, blossom. Josh reaches for the bear and brings its soft black nose to his mouth. The pasta is just about ready.

It is now 5:33 P.M.

And so goes life with two children. One minute you feel completely powerless. A heartbeat later you feel completely blessed. There's chaos, there's joy, exhaustion, and exhilaration. And there's more laundry than ever.

If you've picked up this book, you're either considering adding a new baby to your family mix or the wee one is already on his way. Whatever your current situation. I bet you're feeling a little uncertain about what's to come.

Let's get this out right up front. It's not pretty. At first your life will be a mess, figuratively and quite literally. Feelings will be hurt, sleep will be lost, food will burn. Everyone will feel lonely and neglected at some point.

When the dust settles, however, you will find a new and improved family. Siblings grow into more complex little people. Parents learn that they can, in fact, love another human being as completely as they do their first child. And in a strange, evolutionary kind of way, you may discover how to run your life better.

The question, then, is how long until your family is transformed? As we know, the process of evolution can take millions of years, and most of us just don't have that luxury. So the time to start preparing for this metamorphosis is right now, while the new baby's smaller than a bread box. This book can help you get to that place.

I've called upon parents, doctors, researchers, and children to address a growing family's concerns and expectations. The result? Dozens of tips and practical advice that might help ease this rather bumpy road ahead of you. Throughout this book are suggestions for pampering pregnant bodies, weathering new-baby storms, surviving toddler tantrums, savoring sweet moments, soothing bruised egos, and mending fragile hearts. I sincerely hope that these ideas will help, but not really knowing any of you all that well, I can't guarantee complete success. (As a parent, I try not to make promises I can't keep. There—your first tip.)

Take it from me and the dozens of parents who were kind enough to share their heartfelt stories and anecdotes for this book: The number of children may double, the laundry may increase threefold, and the work may increase sixfold. But none of that will matter as you watch your two children hug for no obvious reason, share a secret, or chase each other, squealing in delight.

Revel in each other.

PART ONE

Planning for Two

That gentle yearning to hold a baby in your arms.

A certain nagging feeling that you're not quite "done" yet.

A desperate desire for another child.

If you have been blessed with one baby and are considering bringing another into your family, you may be experiencing any or all of these sensations. There are perhaps dozens of reasons and a variety of influences that have brought you to this point, many of them out of your hands. You think you know what it takes, but you are full of questions. And although it's been done for ages and ages, it's new to your household. You feel like a pioneer perched on the edge of a new frontier.

It's perfectly reasonable to feel nervous or even ambivalent about this decision—most growing families do. After all, the next step will change the course of your lives in ways you could never imagine. Getting all the facts and understanding what's in store will better prepare you for your expanding role.

Read on, and wagons ho!

Your Changing Family

"Having a child has brought out a whole other side of me that I never really knew was there," says Esther. "I have always enjoyed helping and encouraging people, but the love and care that is bestowed upon a child is far more important and rewarding than anything else I've ever done. We absolutely adore our daughter and wanted to be able to share that love with another child."

It can happen at any time, when you least expect it. It can be part of some grand plan or it could come as a complete surprise. Your threesome is destined to become a moresome.

If this describes your current familial situation, that means you've either decided that you want to try to have another child or, depending on your state of denial, have declared that you are not trying *not* to. Perhaps you are beyond the trying stage and are expecting once again, already sorting old baby clothes and past the Ps in one of those baby-name books.

The mere fact that you are even considering another baby in the house means that you are probably asking yourselves a lot of questions, from "How can I love a second child as much as I adore my first?" to "Will I ever get to see my spouse—awake—again?"

We'll get to those questions and more later in the book. But to start, I'd like to try to answer the most basic question here, "Why have another one?"

When One Is Not Enough

There are a lot of reasons parents decide to fill their houses once again with the smells, sounds, and sweetness of a new baby, although generally, 4:00 A.M. feedings, endless diaper changes, and spit-up around every corner don't top their lists. Rather, a combination of pressures, images, and ideals—and an occasional accident—brings families to the blessed expectant state again.

Family Influences

Many couples form an image of the perfect family size early in their relationships, even before the first one comes along. (Ironically, this is often discussed over coffee in a romantic bistro or while lying in bed talking, two activities that are rarely enjoyed by families with two or more children.) As a matter of fact, individuals may come into relationships with preconceived, so to speak, notions on the topic. What's more, these expectations—for instance, wanting a big, bustling family, or wanting no children whatsoever—may have an impact on the future of the twosome.

A couple's own family backgrounds play a big part in shaping this ideal, researchers report. A 1994 study by the Population Studies Center at the University of Michigan found that a person's own family size (number of siblings), siblings' fertility (the number of nieces and nephews a person has), and parents' offhand remarks about the size of their families (for instance, complaining that they had too many children or that they wished they had more) have an important influence over his family-size preferences. Or, simply put, family size has a tendency to run in families.

"All of my children—William, three; Frank, two; and John, due in October—were entirely planned," explains Pamela. "I am the youngest of six children, and my husband the youngest of four, so large families seem natural to us."

Obviously, not all couples imitate their own families in magnitude, particularly when they harbor particularly trying or harsh memories of their childhoods. For instance, someone who felt lost in a bustling household of siblings may opt for only one or two of their own children. Or an "only" may desire a very different family environment for his own children.

Often, couples report feeling the need to provide grandchildren when other siblings are unable or uninterested. "My sisters have no kids and, at the time, no plans to get married," says Amy, mother to Alice and Caroline, born three years apart. "My husband was an only child and both of his folks were only children. We decided Alice would need reinforcements."

This individual family ideal, however, is subject to modification once the kids start adding up. "Since I'm an only child and my husband's only sibling won't be having any children, we decided we wanted a large family," says Leah, an expectant mother of Jane, a toddler. But when plagued by health problems such as asthma, migraines, and depression during her second pregnancy, Leah and Bill revised their long-term plans. "This will be our last child," she says. "I do not want to be pregnant ever again."

Magic Numbers

Whatever the motivation behind it—growing up in a big family, growing up an only, wanting something better or different for your child—couples often articulate this numerical need as an intuitive sense of what's right for them. "Our second child, Dara, was totally planned, perhaps even overplanned!" says Susan L., referring to the years of fertility-drug treatments and medical procedures she underwent in hopes of conceiving a sibling for her son, Hal. "Our family would not have felt 'complete' without a second child."

It's not uncommon for one parent to feel strongly about increasing the pack when the other has had it with procreating. Says Kathi, "We have two beautiful children, a three-year-old boy and a girl, age one. My husband says we are finished, but I would really like a third. People keep saying, 'Oh, you're so lucky to have one of each, you can be done now,' but I just don't feel like our family is whole yet."

Wendy's idea of the perfect family size doesn't correspond with her husband's, either. "I just don't feel that my 'baby days' are over. We have a seven-year-old boy and a two-and-a-half-year-old girl, but I'm ready for another. My husband thinks we're done, though. Sometimes I wish we had had two of the same sex just because I know he'd give in and try for the other."

Robin decided that her first would be her last just minutes after her daughter was born. "As I was being rolled out of the delivery room after giving birth the first time, I wondered how I was going to tell my husband that this was going to be his only child—by *my* loins anyway! That is how painful labor was for me," she recalls. "But as the months went by, it wasn't so much that I forgot the pain of labor as it was that I grew to love the complexities and mysteries of motherhood. In the first few weeks of my daughter's life I would stare at her in awe, wondering how there could be any room left in my heart for another child. As time went on, I grew to love her so much that I felt I *had* to have a second child. Beth added so much to our lives."

"I really don't know why I want three," says Ashleigh. "That just seems to be the magic number."

Permanent Playmates

Siblings don't take the place of peer relationships outside the home, but they do provide friendship and support and rarely have to be "booked" for fun weeks in advance. Whatever the time or weather, they are a constant in each other's lives, a source of impromptu pillow fights and late-night homework help. Even siblings with a sizable rift in ages discover ways to play together and learn from each other.

While likely, there's no guarantee that two siblings will love and trust each other through the years—in fact, they may avoid each other from the start. But a great many parents appreciate the value of the sibling relationship and embark on a quest to offer that to their children, even when they are not quite convinced that this is what they really want. "I thought it was important for Alex to be able to experience a brother or sister relationship," Michelle explains. "Still, it was a hard decision for us. I worried throughout my whole pregnancy whether we had made the right choice."

Certainly, as time goes on and adolescence approaches, siblings can be instant allies when the inevitable parent-child conflicts erupt. Parents may grudgingly recognize the difference a brother or sister can make. "I always wanted a big family, at least four kids, but after having one child, this seemed unfathomable. My husband, Ed, was so satisfied with Hannah that he said she was enough, maybe we should stop," says Renée. "I reminded Ed that all kids reach a point when they really hate their parents and that it's only fair that we give Hannah a sibling with whom to commiserate. That got him because he has always had special feelings for his sister. So Isaac came along when Hannah was three and a half."

One of Each

The desire for "a matched set" is a common theme among eager parents-to-be. "I love my little girl," says

David, "but I want *ma boy!*" It might be considerably guilt-producing to admit to yourself or your partner that you favor one sex over the other. Typically parents will finish off a statement like that one with, "but as long as it's healthy, I don't care if it's a boy or a girl." Yeah, we know that. But the fact remains, you'll be cheering on those male sperm just the same. (Brief genetics refresher: Both the egg and sperm contain half the genetic blueprint for a little person. As far as whether it turns out to be a boy or girl, the egg doesn't have much say in the matter; eggs always carry the X half of the code. It's therefore up to the sperm to fill in the blank. Lucky for mankind, there are two types of sperm—one carrying an X chromosome, and one that boasts the Y variety. Paired up, XX produces a girl; the XY combo delivers a boy.)

Choose-your-baby's-sex books are exceedingly popular these days, although they give no guarantees. Generally these texts discuss the importance of time, frequency, and positioning of intercourse as they relate to the two types of sperm and their idiosyncrasies. In *How to Choose the Sex of Your Baby: The Method Best Supported by Scientific Evidence*, by Dr. Landrum B. Shettles and David M. Rorvik (Doubleday, 1997), the authors discuss these concepts, the use of ovulation-timing technologies, and various sperm-management techniques such as drinking coffee just before making love if you're hoping for a boy. (Apparently, Y sperm appreciate the caffeine boost.)

Other books on gender preselection include *Boy or Girl?*, by Dr. Elizabeth Whelan (Pocket Books, 1991), and *How to Have a Girl: A Step-By-Step Guide to Scientifically Maximize Your Chances of Conceiving a Daughter* (or its counterpart, *How to Have a Boy*), by J. Martin Young (James Dines & Do., both 1995). For a thoroughly unscientific but fun discussion of the topic, pick up *How to Make a Boy or Girl Baby!: 61 Old Wives' Tales for Determining the Sex of Your Next Child*, by Shelly Lavigne (Dell Books, 1996). Or check out the misc.kids FAQ on choosing your baby's sex at http://www.lib.ox.ac.uk/internet/news/faq/archive/misc-kids.pregnancy.babys-sex.html.

In the end, most parents trying for either a boy or a girl feel blessed to be presented with a healthy, bouncing baby, whatever the sex. If you can both accept that the notion of sex selection is a particularly inexact science, there's nothing wrong with trying to skew the odds a bit. Said one Shettles reader, "When we decided to go ahead with number three, we thought it would be fun to 'try' for a boy. A friend recommended the Shettles book, which I checked out of the library. The book claims eighty percent effectiveness. Apparently we fell into the other twenty percent, which is perfectly fine. I love little girls!"

The "Surprise" Pregnancy

On the other hand, the decision to try for another baby might be out of your hands (not that it ever really is completely in them). You thought you'd have another baby someday, but not *now*. Then again, even if you and your partner were reproductively "winging it," leaving the decision to "chance," you may feel that the timing for this next baby wasn't exactly optimal.

It's normal to feel sad, disappointed, or even a bit guilty when a second pregnancy takes you by surprise. There are a lot of adjustments to be made when a household makes room for one more, but whatever the rough spots, they can be worked through.

"Frankly, I was a little scared when I discovered I was pregnant again," says Joan. "The timing could not have been worse. I had just gone back to work full-time and had received a promotion. We had originally planned on waiting until our first child was two before trying again, but Caroline will only be seventeen months old when this baby arrives. Woops!" As she approached her due date, though, Joan was feeling better about the pregnancy. "At this point I am happy with the idea of baby number two. Somewhere in the last nine months I came to terms with how wonderful a new one, close in age, will be. I figure that it will be nice for the two to grow up together. I realize it will be hard work the first few months, but I think I'm up to it."

As Susan S. also discovered, a tweak to a prior "grand plan" can amount to more happiness than you would have ever expected. "After my first child thirteen years ago, my partner and I were pretty sure we didn't want any more," she says. "After about seven years had passed, we decided maybe we weren't so sure and stopped using birth control. Nothing happened for four years, so I figured that I simply couldn't have any more. I wasn't upset about it, I just figured our original decision had been the right one. In December I missed my period and thought I was pregnant; however, I went for a couple of ultrasounds and was told I had a blighted ovum. I was devastated. I guess I did want another child after all."

Susan and her partner decided to work hard at a new pregnancy and delivered the following December, thinking that would be that. "My partner decided to have a vasectomy, and the next May he did. However, I was six weeks pregnant by then and didn't know it yet!" Susan calls this third pregnancy a blessing in disguise. "The third was totally unplanned, but I had always felt bad that my oldest hadn't had siblings closer in age. For a person who thought she only wanted one child, I've hit the jackpot with my three beautiful girls."

Not So Fast

On the flip side of the second pregnancy that enters without knocking, there are the families that find a subsequent pregnancy frustratingly more elusive than the first. Susan L. and her husband, Peter, became pregnant with their first child, Hal, as fast as reproductively possible. So naturally, when they agreed to try for another baby, they were confused and saddened when one after another, their pregnancies ended in miscarriage. Happily, after six pregnancies in six years of fertility treatments and surgeries, Susan and Peter brought home their much-awaited second child, Dara.

As unlikely as it may sound, there are over a million couples who deal with secondary infertility, defined as the inability to conceive after having established pregnancies (whereas primary infertility describes those who have never been able to achieve a pregnancy). Sue and Peter's ordeal may not fit that definition precisely, yet what they went through is indicative of the many types of problems that can occur without warning. Although many women don't even know the condition exists, secondary infertility is more common statistically than primary infertility. According to the National Center for Health Statistics, more than half of American women who could not conceive or carry a pregnancy to term already had at least one child.

The frustration and disappointment that secondary infertility evokes can have discomforting effects on existing children, particularly if the parents demonstrate significant psychological symptoms such as depression or withdrawal. For help and counsel, contact RESOLVE (1310 Broadway, Somerville, MA 02144–1731; 617–623–0744; http://www.resolve.org/index.htm), a national nonprofit organization that offers information, support, and advocacy for people with fertility problems. RESOLVE offers the fact sheet "Secondary Infertility, Medical & Personal Viewpoints" for a small fee.

Common Concerns

When I began writing this book, I was the mother of one and the mother-to-be of another. I had wanted this baby, wanted two children, wanted my daughter to have as sibling. I welcomed pregnancy, as my first experience had been so positive.

But as my belly grew, so did my apprehensions. Not surprising, since anxiety during a pregnancy is nothing new to parents. During the first, we stay up nights wondering how our lives will change, how our relationships will fare, and how we could possibly be somebody's parents. This time we worry about all of those things, but now we get to stew about how our existing children will adjust.

Expectant again, you may feel plagued by questions and concerns about how the older child will react to the baby and what the new arrival will mean to your relationship with the firstborn. Will he adore his new sibling, or will his entire universe crumble around him? Will there ever be any private time left to spend with the first? If I adore my daughter so much, how could I possibly conjure up any more love for a second?

These concerns are valid, common, and, for the most part, not a cause for alarm. Children are very resilient to change, given support and ongoing love. We adults, on the other hand, tend to be less flexible. Consequently, some of our concerns about having a second child revolve around having to put our own needs and wants on hold.

As you read through these chapters, you'll find dozens of questions that trouble and confound parents-to-be-again. Here, though, are a few of the most common fears keeping expectant parents of two up at night. Do any of these ring a bell?

I'm nervous about how drastically our lives may change. I've heard that going from one child to two is more than twice as hard as adjusting to your first.

First of all, others families' perceptions of the adjustment from one child to two (or more) shouldn't be a barometer for how you and your loved ones will handle it. However, we all ask our friends and colleagues (and for that matter, buy books full of anecdotes from growing families) to get an idea of how the transition *might* play out in our own households. But every family is a mélange of unique personalities, tender bonds, intricate dynamics, and unspoken agendas. Consequently, the rough spots for one family of four (for instance, a bedtime ritual of crying, stalling, waking, and whining that goes on for hours) may not apply to a well-rested but hard-to-mobilize (especially in the morning) household.

Says Kim, mother of a three-year-old and a two-monther, "I found that going from one to two so far has been much, much easier than I expected. My daughter wasn't nearly as horrified as I had anticipated, and the second child has been much easier going than the first—perhaps because we're calmer as parents." In Kim's opinion, the smooth transition from one child to two has a lot to do with her husband, Rick, and his participation as a parent. "Rick does a lot of our child care and always has. Even though I do the bulk of it, he's very realistic about things and fair-minded—always willing to let me have some 'selfish' time to myself if I need it, things like that. I think that with two, both parents definitely wind up doing a lot of things, so that if the second parent isn't already used to that or is unrealistic about it, it can create a lot of friction when the second child comes along."

Won't a new baby "ruin" the relationship I have with my first child?

"My son and I were such pals, we did everything together," says Claire. "When I was pregnant with my second, I thought that I was going to ruin our wonderful close relationship. I cried more for him than for anything else that was going on."

There is validity to the notion that a new baby scuffs the mother-child relationship somewhat. A study by researchers at the University of Maryland investigated the "attachment security" of preschoolers to their mothers, in effect the quality of the parent-child relationship, just before a new baby entered the household and a few months after the birth. It probably doesn't surprise you to hear that yes, the transition to siblinghood and the disruption of the parent-child relationship is stressful for children. What's more, of the children studied, those age two through five had a much harder time adjusting than those under twenty-four months. This may be because the ability of any child to feel threatened and displaced by a new baby requires more social and cognitive development than that achieved by children under age two. And it's quite possible that younger firstborns may display the stronger negative reactions demonstrated by older children once they reach age two.

In a somewhat vicious circle, the older child's reactions to the new baby, whether anxiety, feelings of displacement, anger, clinginess, whininess, sleep disturbances, and/or aggression, may have a detrimental effect on the quality of the parent-child relationship, researchers say. These problematic behaviors may lead mothers to spend less time or express more negativity and "controlling interactions" with the firstborn as they attempt to cope with a new baby's demands.

If you can recognize how you react to your first child's response to the new baby, then you may get a better handle on your own actions. In turn, you may possibly ease the transition from only to big sibling. For instance, scolding a child for whining when you sit down to breast-feed is almost guaranteed to lock you into a downward spiral of crying, yelling, and fussing that can last an afternoon. Instead, try to appreciate why your child isn't all that thrilled about you snuggling with this new kid, and keep your voice steady, reassuring, and positive. You may steer him away from the whiny zone and as a result you'll be enjoying his company more than you might have.

So when your two-year-old refuses to acknowledge your presence for a few days, or your three-year-old refuses to drink from any cup you offer her, remember that they are fragile little people struggling with perhaps the most difficult situation they've ever endured. Keep in mind all that you love about them even if they seem impossible to love.

The impact of a new sibling may seem at first challenging to the bonds you share. Your child's time as an "only" has ended, but a new phase of his life will be beginning. Remarkably, you'll form unique bonds with each child, and find ways to feel "close" with each of them.

How will I have enough time to spend with each child?

In a perfect world (and put down this book right now if that is where you're reading this from) there would be plenty of time for everything we wanted or needed to do. But hello, and welcome to Earth, where time is as precious as the children we don't see enough.

When parents work (and indeed, someone has to), there are only a few hours in each day to be savored by family members en masse. And unfortunately, since a good part of that time gets taken up with chores or errands, it may seem like there's not even enough quality time for one young 'un.

"Lack of time was probably my biggest concern about having a second baby," says Larry. "It seemed like all of our time was already being taken up by one child, with none left over for us as a couple or for me individually. How could we possibly have enough time for another baby?"

Sorry to break it to you, but you won't. The days won't get longer (although it might seem that way), and the demands will be greater, I promise you. On the other hand, you will get better at managing the time you have. You will find ways to attend to your children's needs that won't involve cloning yourself or hiring a staff. The trick is to not punish yourself for being singular.

"My children are twenty-nine months apart and I worried a lot about not giving them the individual attention they needed. So I make sure that I have some time alone with each of them to do special things," Anna explains. "For instance, I take my daughter to a mommy-and-me class each week, just the two of us. My son stays up much later than my daughter, so we also get time alone. Together they are wonderful; she squeals in delight when she sees him, and he is her big protector. I wouldn't have it any other way."

As for personal time, it may seem elusive for a while, but for the most part it's a temporary setback. After months or years of having a small chunk of time to yourself to rejuice—whether that was after your first child went to bed or while your spouse or partner looked after him—you may find that a new baby tends to soak up that overflow time like a thirsty, needy sponge. So often, when one of you is bathing or playing with the older child, the other finds himself rocking or cuddling the baby. But if your older child has good bedtime and sleeping habits, chances are that your new baby will conform to a similar pattern in a few months or so.

Obviously the "divide and conquer" technique doesn't lend itself well to couple enrichment. You may have to work harder at finding time alone—hiring sitters, appreciating stolen moments. Again, it's a relatively temporary situation. There will always be needs and feelings to juggle, but the baby *will* grow out of the intense phase and you will settle into a routine of sorts.

Those first six weeks were hard enough with one baby around. Will we get any sleep when there are two in the house?

In the first month of a newborn's life, sleep becomes a rare commodity for the entire family. Your baby may awaken every two or three hours around the clock. Plus, your older child is likely to experience a few sleep disturbances of his own, whether he has trouble settling in at night, starts waking up early, or demands your attention whenever the baby wakes up to feed.

"By far, the hardest part about the first six weeks was the lack of sleep," says Jeanette. "Cody nursed and fussed almost constantly, and when he did get quiet, Ben would wake him up again. It was so frustrating. A good day was one in which both of them napped at the same time. I might even get a chance to take a shower then."

This, too, shall pass. In Jeanette's household, things "seemed to fall into a routine quickly." If you don't encourage your older child's midnight rousings by offering snacks or reading books during the night, he may soon tire of the sport and come to appreciate the warmth and coziness of his bed after all. Likewise, minimize the amount of stimulation your baby gets during the night by keeping lights low during feedings and by avoiding the TV if you can. Nurse or bottle-feed in the baby's room and return him to his crib quickly.

Partners should practice tag-team sleeping if possible. My husband always used to get upset if, on the nights or early mornings he tended the baby, I got up along with him. I couldn't help it, I loved to watch them together. However, he had a valid point. One of you should savor sleep when the other cannot, since, at some later time, that well-rested soul will be better able to take charge of the kids while the other catches a refresher.

Getting as much rest yourself as you possibly can will help you better deal with toddler meltdowns and other hazards of parenting two, so sneak in naps whenever feasible. You may not always be able to "sleep when baby sleeps" since other children don't abide by this rule, but you can enlist neighbors or relatives to give a child-caring hand in the early days.

Won't a new baby shatter my firstborn's world as he knows it?

A dramatic way to phrase it, but yes. Since your family is the center of your child's world, allowing another small person into the mix will be disturbing to him. Change is not always a bad thing, however, and a child's ability to cope with this wrinkle in the fabric of his life depends on your ability to soothe and smooth.

It may take a few days or weeks, but your child will come to realize that all the things he holds familiar and dear—preschool, toys, gymnastics classes, neighborhood friends—are still exactly where he left them. Most important, so are you. Without a doubt, you will need to offer extra hugs and unsolicited kisses every day, to remind him of your unconditional love. This goes for cranky days, nasty days, even days spent mostly in the "uncooperative chair." (Read *Julius, the Baby of the World*, by Kevin Henkes, and you'll understand.)

Preparing him for the changes well ahead of time can also lessen the "shattering" effects of bringing home a new family member. Read, read, read about babies and siblings. Talk about all the things a baby will need and what his new role will be. And never stop stressing that the baby isn't going to take anyone's place, but is a joyous gift that the whole family will need to tend to and to love.

2

Are You Ready?

"We weren't completely prepared for our second child, but we are both excited about the prospect of another baby," says Carol. "We're worried about our finances, but confident that will all work out. We just pray for a healthy, happy baby."

To think that we can "time" a child to correspond with downtime in a job, finishing a home-improvement project, or waiting until an older child is emotionally ready is a tad unrealistic. Sure, you might shun the idea within weeks of one child's birth or during rough financial times. But in broader terms, we can't necessarily conceive children, or for that matter adopt a child, exactly when we want them any more than we can predict what will be happening in our lives nine months or more down the line. A quick conception and easy pregnancy the first time doesn't guarantee anything about pregnancies to come. On the other hand, what took seasons last time might be accomplished in a romantic weekend away.

What's more, sometimes babies don't wait to be invited. They burst into our lives "unplanned" and ready to party. "This baby was a total surprise. A shock. An unbelievable twist in our lives," says Sheri, whose firstborn is in junior high. Other seconds hold back for the grand entrance, making their parents wish and wait and hope for months or years. A lot fall somewhere in between, just in time for a big promotion, a family dilemma, or your toddler's first attempts at potty learning.

Perfect Timing

If everyone waited for the perfect time to have a baby, there would probably be a lot fewer of us around. No time is best for expanding your family; however, there are certain criteria, such as good health, financial stability, and being part of a loving relationship, that, if met, could considerably ease some of the challenges that a new baby can bring.

Looking back at your first pregnancy, you may wonder how you ever felt that you were ready for such a major life change. Indeed, going from a couple to a family can be a tumultuous transition, as you and your partner find yourselves stepping into new roles and sometimes losing yourselves in the process. But if you've been through that already, gaining another family member will be less of an ego jolt, right? Been there, done that.

You and your partner have gotten used to thinking of yourselves as parents, and hey, you're pretty darn good at it. You are both seasoned nurturers, you love each other, and you think you've always wanted to have more than one kid. Does this mean that you're ready to try again? Not necessarily. There are a great many variables to address this time, and they are not all related to you. This time there's an existing child's personality and adaptability to consider. Ask yourselves the following questions and share your answers with each other. You may find that one of you isn't as sure as you thought, or you may discover that the time has never been better.

The Tough Questions

Whether you use this discussion to plan a new pregnancy or you are already expecting as you read this, these questions can guide you toward creating strategies for strengthening your relationship, solidifying your commitments, and building a better future for your family.

Do you both want to have another baby?

Maybe you've known from the minute you held your first child in your arms that you wouldn't want to stop there. Or maybe you feel pressure from your partner to have another baby, but given the choice, you would wait a year or two more. Ask yourself, honestly, why you think you want another child and try to envision what your family life would be like after he or she has been born. Share your expectations of each other in this expanded family and make sure that they are compatible.

Have you spent enough alone time with your first child?

There's no expert or statistical answer to this one; rather, it's how you feel about the time that you have spent with your child so far. Maybe you've been working sixty-hour weeks for most of your young child's life, and feel that what time you have left each week with her just isn't quite enough. Well, be aware that a new baby will definitely cut into those precious moments with the older one. Moreover, parents don't like to think that a new baby will hinder their relationship with their first child, but the introduction of a sibling might spur behavior problems in the first, making your time with her less enjoyable.

As bad as that might sound, it may be harder for you

than for the children. The older child may have less one-on-one time with you, but it's not as if the concept will be out of the question for the next twenty years. There are ways to spend alone time with each. There are also the benefits of having a sibling and being part of a bigger family, which can be even more enriching than time alone with you. And already the second child got to have you to himself for a few years—none of your other children will ever be able to make *that* claim.

Are your finances up to the challenge?

Considering doctor's bills, clothing, feeding supplies, bedding, and diapers, a new baby will cost approximately five thousand dollars in the first year. Child-care fees, toys, Beanie Babies, and other necessities inflate the total. Of course, you don't have to be financially solvent to have another baby, but having a steady and dependable source of income will ensure a healthy, stable, and less stressful environment for all of your children. Not to mention the fact that there are still gymnastics lessons, karate classes, bar mitzvahs, college tuitions, and weddings down the road cheerily waiting to send you their bills.

"I seem to get 'provider anxiety' with each baby," explains Mike, father of three. "That is, as the number of children increases, I get concerned that I should be making more money, providing more security. A particular factor with the third: I felt that at this point my wife should be able to completely stop working if she wanted to—and that meant the entire financial responsibility was on me, not just for current expenses but saving for college, a larger house, and more."

Child care is a financial issue as well as an emotional concern for parents of two or more kids. "Paying for two in day care will be difficult," says Bill. "And since we don't want to send the new baby to a day-care situation right away, my wife will be forced to take the bulk of the care responsibilities—a problem since she wants and needs to go back to work sooner." As the child-care fees mount with each child, parents may need to rethink their current strategy (for instance, day-care center versus a nanny).

This is an excellent time to work out a budget for your growing family and stick to it. A software program such as Quicken Deluxe (800–224–0991; http://www.qfn.com) or Microsoft Money (800–368–5351; http://www.microsoft.com/money/) can help you track your expenses, organize your finances, and plan for the future. You might also consider consulting with a professional financial planner to discuss debt reduction or how to optimize your investments to fit your changing needs.

Do you have room for two?

Certainly many of us grew up sharing a bedroom with a sibling, and your children can survive it as well. In fact, some families actually prefer to keep the kids together and leave a third bedroom available for playtime or for guests—and the children wouldn't have it any other way.

But the idea of having room enough for two kids extends beyond the bedroom. They'll need sleeping space, of course, but there are also high chairs, baby toys, toddler toys, and so on. Remember, as your children get bigger, their "stuff" grows and accumulates proportionately.

In their bedroom and their play areas, you'll need to pay particular attention to baby-proofing. A toddler or preschooler's room can instantly become strewn with bite-size action-figure accessories or the daintiest of doll shoes. Assuming he's old enough, your first child will need to become your ally in the war against choking hazards. But if he's a bit young to be diligent about such things, he's either too young for small pieces himself or probably won't mind sticking to chunkier toys for a few more months.

How's your energy level?

Does your first child tire you out? Is it all you can do to keep up with their soccer games, school plays, and Gymboree classes? Or do you find your interactions with your child energizing and uplifting?

Ironically, tiring out quickly from a game of catch with your preschooler may not mean you're doing too much, but rather that you're not doing enough. Getting regular exercise will help you have more energy for family fun. You'll also sleep more soundly, concentrate better, and may take the inevitable sibling conflicts in stride once you get those happy endorphins pumping.

Finding the time to work out can be a challenge with children in the house, but it can be done. Take a brisk walk or use a treadmill before your child wakes up. Walk or take an exercise class during your lunch hour. Trade off exercise-designated child-care responsibilities with your partner; for instance, go to step aerobics on Tuesday night, and let him play racquetball on Thursday night. Or just *play* with your child, every day if you can—swing, run, blow bubbles, throw a ball, ride your bikes.

If you are planning or currently in a pregnancy, check with your doctor before beginning a new exercise program. Unless you have had signs of preterm labor, incompetent cervix, persistent bleeding, or complications such as pregnancy-induced hypertension, she'll most likely give you the green light to get moving. Be sure to wear appropriate clothing, drink fluids throughout the workout, and eat a nutritious diet.

How would a new baby affect your career(s)?

For working parents, a second child often means more sick days, doctor's appointments, field trips, soccer games. There's also a lot more guilt: about the games you couldn't make, about the time you're missing with your child, about not putting in 200 percent at the office. Something has to give. If you are staying in a current full-time position, you may want to travel less or take on fewer duties. Sometimes that means missed opportunities for advancement or not enough time to finish your projects.

Some parents who worked after a first child arrived may make a more radical decision, such as cutting back drastically or staying home full-time, when the second child enters the picture. Financially it might not make sense if day care times two obliterates one partner's salary or if it's more or less a wash. But don't burn any bridges until you're sure this is right for you. If you are considering the possibility of leaving work completely, is that a reasonable option? Or is a part-time position more logical? "After working for ten years, I'm not sure I could stay home all day with my kids and keep them and myself happy," explains Mary-Austin. "I think part-time would give me the ability to spend more time with my children, yet have the interactions I love in the adult world."

How would another baby affect travel or leisure plans?

Just as you find more travel opportunities opening up for you and your maturing child, the addition of a baby puts you right back into the slow lane. That's not to say that a new baby will ground you completely, because certainly there are family resorts, campgrounds, cruise lines, and even select Club Meds that welcome wee ones.

There are some destinations and activities that are not particularly baby-friendly, and they will have to wait. But weigh that against time nurturing your growing family, and you'll realize that these wild adventures will still be an option when your baby can better appreciate them. "We haven't had a real vacation in a long time, but frankly, I would rather have children year-round than spend a week in Hawaii each year. We'll get to that when they're older," says Pamela, mother of two, with one on the way.

Is your relationship fit for two?

Think back to the early days with your first newborn. How did you and your partner weather the demands as a team? Were you able to convey each other's needs well and respond accordingly? Or did the added pressures of parenthood cause a rift in your previous relationship? Are you a better couple now than before your first pregnancy?

Those first few weeks are hard on any relationship; however, if there were significant rough spots with the first—say, one of you not doing your share of baby-care duties, or a lack of communication about each other's needs during that time—now is the time to discuss them and work them through. If aspects of your relationship have changed drastically since then, don't wait until the baby arrives to address these issues.

If you are part of a stepfamily, raising a newborn might be a novel venture for you as conspirators. That means you face your first time together as parents of a newborn—a trying time at best—but you may also have other children to boot. Now is the time to discuss your expectations of each other in the postpartum days and further down the road. And even if one of you has been there before, it's a good idea to take a childbirth preparation class together.

Adding Everything Up

Confronting these issues may have raised even more questions. That's a good thing. This isn't a test out of *Cosmopolitan* magazine; the goal here is not to score one hundred points and a free trip to your bedroom. It's to get you thinking about all the concerns in your life that will be impacted by a new baby. And once you've considered them at length, you can begin to prioritize your goals and needs.

Maybe you want to wait until your one-year-old turns three before trying for a second. Plus, you've also been saving for a home. But career-wise, this would be the year to take a short break, perfect for family leave. Emotionally, you want a baby tomorrow.

On which of these issues are you most flexible? Could you put off a home purchase for a couple of years, if need be? Or could you reconsider the age gap? Be truthful with yourself and then share this with your partner. Whether this pregnancy is planned, timed, or completely unforeseen, you need to be honest with each other about what this means to yourselves, your futures, your children, the family you are becoming. Left unspoken, unresolved issues tend to fester unattractively. When they're brought into the daylight, we get the chance to strengthen the bonds we share.

3

Planning a Sibling Strategy

"My sister was, and still is, my best friend," says Carmen, born less than two years apart from her sibling. "Day to day it didn't always seem that way, but when I think about the big picture, she was always there for me. I know it will be hard for me having two babies so close in age, but I can make a few small sacrifices if it means my children might share such a special bond."

Parents may fantasize about their children playing together, supporting each other, and being best friends as they grow up. Indeed, many families report that a key reason in bringing a second baby into their household was to provide a peer for their existing child so that the firstborn wouldn't have to grow up "alone."

But when these parents embark on such a long-term play date, they are helping to shape their children's futures in ways that are extremely complex. As siblings, children learn to share their parents and their possessions. Older children in particular get to experience teaching, caregiving, managing, and helping roles for perhaps the first time. Siblings watch and learn from each other. And as they occur, these interactions lay the groundwork for relationships they will experience later in life, according to Susan Scarf Merrell, author of *The Accidental Bond: The Power of Sibling Relationships* (Times Books, 1995).

"With our siblings, to some extent, we actually play out our first 'marriages,' " Merrell writes. "We experience conflicting yearnings for enmeshment and independence; we learn how to argue, negotiate, and compromise; how to express affection and to balance our need for privacy with our need for closeness. We learn what behavior is appropriate with peers, and what is not. And as we interact, react, and develop, the essential elements of our personalities evolve as well."

As enriching and valuable as the sibling connection may be, your thoughts when planning for a second child may not focus immediately on the positive aspects, but rather the conflicts and keen competition that seemingly pervade every sibling relationship. Such "sibling rivalry" brings to mind images of angry, jealous, even vengeful brothers and sisters. Realistically, however, when handled properly, healthy competition among siblings can lead to the acquisition of social, interpersonal, and cognitive skills that are imperative to a child's development.

Sibling Struggles

For as long as there have been siblings, there has been sibling rivalry. Cain and Abel, Jacob and Esau, and Joseph and his brothers vied for their parents' love, affection, attention, and recognition, and your children will as well. However, don't let the concept of sibling rivalry, as confrontational as it may sound, scare you away from taking the next step. Dealt with intelligently, sibling rivalry in your own family can produce far better than biblical consequences.

In *Siblings Without Rivalry: How to Help Your Children Live Together So You Can Live Too*, by Adele Faber and Elaine Mazlish (Avon, 1987), the authors tout the benefits of sibling conflicts. From their struggles to establish dominance over each other, they write, siblings become tougher and more resilient. From the endless roughhousing they develop speed and agility. From their verbal sparring they learn the difference between being clever and being hurtful. From the normal irritations of living together they learn how to assert themselves, defend themselves, and compromise. And sometimes, from the envy of each other's special abilities, they become inspired to work harder, persist, and achieve.

These are the best things about rivalry, the authors say. However, the negative implications of sibling struggles can impact a person's entire life. Parental mismanagement of the competition—by taking sides in conflicts, continually blaming the older child, or not letting children work through their problems constructively—may lead to psychological problems later in life. Constant comparisons of siblings' intellect, physical appearance, or achievements, for example, can be detrimental to a child's self-esteem. The resulting feelings of anger, jealousy, and resentment can be carried into adult relationships. The child may grow up to be selfish, aggressive, destructive, indecisive, or insecure.

Dr. T. Berry Brazelton, who has written extensively on sibling rivalry, defends the notion that rivalry can be a beneficial learning experience for involved siblings, but cautions that the triangle of child–interfering parent–child keeps it alive as a negative experience. "A positive relationship between the children can never take place when the parent steps in to interfere," Brazelton writes in *Toddlers and Parents: A Declaration of Independence* (Dell, 1989). Rushing in to choose sides or immediately comfort the child who cries loudest simply reinforces the rivalry, he says. By letting children work through their differences on their own, it is much more likely the conflict will end in positive play together.

The Roots of Rivalry

Adolescents vying for athletic awards, school honors, or parental recognition are what parents commonly imagine as sibling rivalry scenarios. Yet sibling rivalry goes deeper than winning medals or achieving good grades. The root of sibling jealousy, write Faber and Mazlish, is each child's deep desire for the exclusive love of his parents. "Siblings threaten everything that is essential to a child's well-being. The mere existence of an additional child or children in the family could signify *less*. Less time alone with parents. Less attention for hurts and disappointments. Less approval for accomplishments."

Sibling rivalry, then, is so much more than a tug-of-war over a Barney puppet or a race down the driveway. It can begin before the younger child can run or tug, even before he can babble or smile. In fact, rivalry may erupt in the moments a new baby comes through the front door—if not before. The perceived loss of parental affection a new baby may inflict may cause a sibling to react with rejection or hate toward the little "intruder." He may feel displaced because of the parents' preoccupation with the new baby and the lack of attention from his mom and dad as well as visitors to the house.

When a baby comes home, the older child may become hostile toward the new family member or may even deny his existence. He may offer what he perceives as helpful suggestions, such as returning the baby to the hospital or to mommy's tummy, or flushing it down the toilet. He may demand attention from whichever parent is currently occupied with the baby, particularly during breast-feeding. And although serious abuse by siblings is rare, he may hit, punch, push, kick, or bite the young child.

Generally, a rough ride is to be expected. Regressive behavior, such as bed-wetting, thumb-sucking, temper tantrums, excessive crying, or quietness is a common manifestation of sibling rivalry. In a study of twenty-one firstborn children with new babies, the vast majority demonstrated some form of regressive behavior. One study, for instance, reported an increase in behavioral problems in 92 percent of thirty-one firstborn children after the birth of a second child. And interestingly, such jealous or hos-

tile feelings may be displaced onto family pets, other play-
mates, or inanimate objects such as toys.

What's more, children can be ingenious in their plots
to draw you away from the baby. Say, for instance, you
are attempting to eat a family dinner when the ten-month-
old begins to cry. Mother begins to offer him pieces of
bread or bits of chicken. Dad chimes in with a suggestion
of cheese or some applesauce. Mom gets up to fetch those.
All this time, the three-year-old is wondering what she
can do to get so much attention. This is usually about the
time her potatoes sail across the room or she decides to
make "chicken soup" out of her plate of food using her
cup of chocolate milk.

It doesn't seem to matter to older siblings how much
they horrify, frighten, anger, or disgust you. He may flush
mail down the toilet, dump out the garbage pail, wrap
his dirty socks around his neck, or hand the baby's last
diaper to the dog. What counts is that he won you away
from the little stinker.

A nightmarish image, don't you think? Yet it's fairly
typical. And the kicker is that parents need to keep their
cool in these situations—no yelling, no screaming. As
Brazelton writes, expecting a child to give up on wanting
your attention is missing the point. "It's not the child's
fault for demanding too much from you. You can't blame
him for his needs." Overreacting may only further his
anxieties and reinforce his demanding ways.

Giving Them Space

With such powerful consequences, it's no wonder parents
agonize over the "perfect" spacing of their children. By
waiting for a certain minimum amount of space, they try
to minimize competition among siblings and to give each
child a chance to enjoy his babyhood. "We wanted to try
to space the second baby close to three years after the

first if we possibly could. It worked out almost to the month," Kim remarked two weeks before her second baby was due. "The timing has been great. In fact, my daughter, for the first time in her life, is showing signs of healthy separation from me. She's asking for her dad more and more, enjoying playing with him. She sometimes wants to play in her room without me, things like that. I'm sure she'll regress somewhat after the baby comes, but I feel it is better to start from this point than from a needy, dependent stage."

For some folks, on the other hand, only a larger span would do. "My son and his sister are six years apart—a huge gap at times, but we wouldn't have had it any other way," Dawn admits. "I could never have handled two in diapers at once."

There are a lot of theories about the best time to introduce a new baby to the household. But the truth is, whatever age your sibling-to-be may be, it's going to be a challenge in some way. There are pros and cons to every age span. Figuring out what's "right" for your family depends a lot on your personalities and your lifestyle.

Two Under Two

Siblings who are this close in age have a lot going for them: They have more in common, may enjoy many of the same games and activities, and can share friends and toys. There are perks for parents as well: If you are planning to stop at two, you get all the diapers and bottles over with in as short a span as possible. Vacations, careers, and educational goals that were put on hold for the "childbearing years" will be in sight sooner rather than later.

Compact as the childbearing years may be, they will be tough. Raising two kids under two is very attention-intensive. Between raising the kids, going to work, and tending to the house, there may not be much time left over for the little things that mattered with a first child, such as sending out birth announcements or filling up photo albums. As Regina explains, "I've hardly taken any pictures of Julia," her three-month-old. On the other hand, Laura, Julia's fifteen-month-old sibling, boasts an over-filled, beautiful book of photographs from the same time period. At press time, Regina was more concerned with getting a chance to shower than arranging mementoes.

For the same reason that kids this close in age have the potential to become great friends and confidants, the rivalry between them can be extremely intense. Similar interests and similar goals may make them prone to hurt feelings as they grow up.

The good news about this age span is that the earliest days with two under two may be easier than with other age differences. Research shows that children under twenty-four months have an easier time adjusting to a new brother or sister than those over age two, probably because they are too young to understand the implications of a new baby in the house. But that doesn't mean you're out of the woods: Once these children figure out what went down, they may begin to act up.

Remember, though they may seem to share toys and interests, they are two completely different individuals at different stages in their lives. Don't forget to treat them that way.

Toddlers and Preschoolers

The most common age gap among children, two to four years is usually cited by parents as the "perfect" gap. The older child is learning new skills that can better equip him to cope with the stresses of a new baby: gaining more control over his body and his language, learning to assert his independence, gaining friends and confidence. He may attend preschool or gymnastics classes, and have a variety of favorite activities and interests.

However, a child who is two to four years old may feel the effects of sibling jealousy most severely. He's old enough to understand that there's an "intruder" in the house but not completely confident in your unconditional, boundless love. Involving the firstborn with the pregnancy and with the newborn, and making sure that he gets his fair share of attention, can help ease his transition. The first few weeks can be tumultuous, but a child in this age range can quickly learn that getting involved with the new baby is a terrific way to get your attention and praise. Although it might take a while, the child can eventually begin to understand that your love won't go away because of the new baby and that everyone has an important role in the family. "We thought that two years was a good space for our girls. Hopefully it will give them enough distance not to put me in the nuthouse and enough closeness to be good friends as well as sisters," says Leah Ann.

Although siblings in this age range can potentially enjoy activities together, it's essential that parents respect their differences and avoid "clumping" them together too often. While you may consider your three-year-old and six-month-old close in age, your firstborn may be considering herself a "big kid" relative to the baby. Make sure that they each have access to age-appropriate toys and activities. Go ahead and praise the older child for helping to soothe or amuse the baby, but don't force her. There will be time for sharing secrets later on.

School Age on Up

Once kids get closer to school age, rivalry is less of an issue. Babies are no longer perceived as a threat, and the firstborn has more important concerns to attend to. What's more, studies have shown that wide spacing of children has been found to be beneficial for the intellectual development of both the younger and older siblings. In this situation the transition may be harder on the parent, who has to get used to diapers and sleepless nights after all these years.

Susan L. noticed relatively little regression, jealousy, or

emotional disturbances in her son, Hal, age five when sister Dara was born. "I think that the age difference is a significant factor. Although we never planned to have them this far apart in age, it works really well. They are constantly at different stages and can be enjoyed as individuals. Hal is mature enough that he is a helper rather than a hindrance. The only thing that is made more difficult by the age difference is deciding where to go on vacation, and finding activities that they both can enjoy."

A span of four or more years doesn't mean that jealousy will be nonexistent, though. Your first child was an "only" for so long that it might be hard for her to give up her throne. But by this age, at least, she's developed the cognitive and emotional tools that can help her work through these conflicting emotions.

Rather than plan your baby according to a predetermined age difference (indeed, pregnancies are not often planned, nor do they bless us precisely when we hope they will), it's better to examine your firstborn's personality and temperament and decide on the best way to handle his promotion to big siblinghood. An adaptable, easygoing preschooler may prove a happier sibling than an older child who is insecure about herself and her parents' love. Children who can identify and verbalize their feelings are also likely to deal with a step up to siblinghood well.

However many grades separate our children, they will profoundly affect each other's lives in ways that we could never imagine. We hope they will lend each other friendship, support, love, and approval—and we can do what we can to encourage that. But ultimately, the spacing of our children, as well as how they relate to one another, will rely on biological happenstance and the fit of their two unique personalities. Eventually we'll need to stand aside.

SOURCES ON SIBLINGS

- *The Accidental Bond: The Power of Sibling Relationships*, by Susan Scarf Merrell (Times Books, 1995)

- *Loving Each One Best: A Caring and Practical Approach to Raising Siblings*, by Nancy Samalin with Catherine Whitney (Bantam Doubleday Dell, 1997)

- *The Sibling Bond*, by Stephen Bank and Michael D. Kahn (HarperCollins, 1997)

- *Sibling Relationships Across the Life Span*, by Victor Cicirelli (Plenum, 1995)

- *Siblings Without Rivalry: How to Help Your Children Live Together So You Can Live Too*, by Adele Faber and Elaine Mazlish (Avon, 1987)

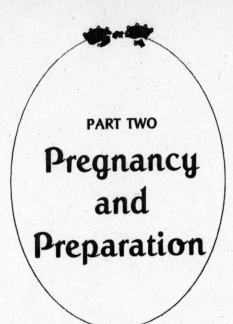

PART TWO

Pregnancy and Preparation

The wheels are in motion, and your new, expanded family is just months away—although it will seem like mere weeks. You may not swoon over every little flutter your fetus grants you; in fact, there may be days you spend so much time chasing your toddler that you forget you are pregnant! With less time to daydream, the days go much faster.

Throughout this fleeting time, it's important to include your firstborn on the discussions and preparations as often as it seems reasonable. He should always feel that this will be his baby too. Letting him in on the activities and excitement will reassure his importance in the family.

As for the pregnancy and birth, assume nothing. Accept that the cravings will be different. Your energy level will be different. Morning sickness is as likely as the first time. And labor may be quicker. But most important, don't count on a baby shower this time around!

That said, let's take a closer look at the nine months—and the exhilarating grand finale—ahead.

4

Same Body, Different Baby

"The second pregnancy was a relative breeze," says Kim. "I think the fact that I had to tend to my daughter and wasn't able to focus so much on myself helped me get through it all much more easily."

A pregnant woman who has been there before might think she knows what to expect. If that's the case, she's in for nine months of surprises.

From a physical point of view, second pregnancies aren't mere replays of those first nine months. You are dealing with a completely different collection of fetal cells and fluids this time—the one constant in the pregnancy equation in your uterus. However, your womb is now more accustomed to getting stretched, kicked, and contorted, and, if you're lucky, may repeat the performance with less of a grumble.

You may have so much false labor that the hospital personnel get to know you by your first name. There may be new aches and sharper pains. The baby may drop sooner, lodging himself so deep into your pelvis weeks before delivery that even the thought of transition seems preferable to walking around this way. Possibly things may go more smoothly than your first pregnancy: You might escape morning sickness or be spared a complication that grounded you last time.

Emotionally, you may find the highs and lows of this pregnancy strikingly different from the first. You are a different person now—a mother, a parent, a pregnancy survivor. You are not easily fazed by fetal kicks, persistent heartburn, or the threat of Pitocin. On the other hand, you are utterly moved by your toddler whispering to your belly, "I love you, little baby." Have Kleenex on hand.

Most women are more relaxed about the pregnancy itself, focusing less on the minor physical twinges than on the worries about the new baby's effect on her other children. What's more, simple day-to-day parenting concerns leave little time for fretting over such pregnancy minutiae as itchy bellies and tired feet.

What to Expect . . . This Time

The second pregnancy may be easier or tougher, similar in some ways, and totally different in others. From the first wave of nausea that heralds a fetus' existence to the labor and birth, each pregnancy, like the child it produces, has its own personality, its own likes and dislikes, its own story to tell.

Out in Front

For some women, the entire experience is better than they remember; for others, it's only bigger. Don't be surprised if you are sporting maternity clothes before your twelfth week; while you might be just getting used to the idea of being pregnant, from your tummy's point of view, it's "show time!"

A quicker gain in girth doesn't necessarily signal a diet problem, and it certainly doesn't mean you'll get fatter this time. Simply put, abdominal muscles that have been stretched in a first pregnancy rarely regain the tone and resistance they had previously. So in a second pregnancy, the roundness returns much faster.

Because your muscles are looser, you may take on a different silhouette than you did with your first, carrying lower or farther out than before. Connie remembers carrying her first child, Stephanie, "very high. After birth, I had three bruised ribs." But her son, Joshua, preferred to lie low, so far down, in fact, that "it hurt to walk after the sixth month."

The Return of the Saltine

Predicting whether you'll experience morning sickness is about as easy as predicting your baby's future career choice. "During the first, I experienced only a bit of routine discomfort," says one mom. "With the second, I was blessed with a full helping of everything—nausea, morning sickness, heartburn—throughout the entire nine months. Even though the morning sickness lessened in the last half of my second pregnancy, it never truly disappeared."

"The only pregnancy that I was really sick with was the first one," Brenda, a mother of five, recalls. "I think that was because I miscarried at about nine weeks. My next pregnancy wasn't too bad, and each pregnancy got a little easier in terms of morning sickness. With each pregnancy, though, there was something that I couldn't eat. With my eldest daughter, it was eggs. With my son I conceived in September, the smell of turkey cooking at Thanksgiving sent me over the edge. Then I couldn't eat it for months!"

If you are among the queasy, the same advice given to first-timers with morning sickness applies now: Eat several small meals rather than three large ones, and avoid anything that has to do with foods that make you nauseated. (Let your partner cook the eggs for your three-year-old, if that turns your stomach.) Make sure your doctor is aware that you are feeling ill, particularly if you are throwing up frequently. It doesn't take long to become severely dehydrated, which can pose risks to you and your fetus and may bring on preterm labor.

Aches and Pains

Stretching ligaments, loosening joints, and other muscular effects of pregnancy can be more pronounced the second time around, since many of these areas have been "primed" already. "Both pregnancies were very easy," said Michelle. "However, with my second I had a lot of pelvic pain that I hadn't experienced with my first. Some days it was really difficult to walk or to get any sleep."

Stooping to pick up toddlers and their many accoutrements can wreak havoc with a pregnant woman's back, so make an effort to lift correctly (with a straight back, bending at the knees) and don't push it. Getting some sort of exercise each day can help keep muscles and joints toned and limber—walking and swimming are particularly kind to expectant bodies. You might also want to look into working out with other pregnant women in a class environment: dance, aerobics, even yoga.

Swifter Kicks

Expectant moms may think they're getting punted earlier than they did in their first pregnancies. More likely, though, the difference is not the timing of the kicks but in the mothers' ability to decipher them. In a first pregnancy, women might mistake early fetal flutters, or *quickening*, for last night's tacos up until about eighteen weeks—a point when there's usually little doubt about what she's feeling. But once a woman has experienced quickening, a second-time mother can identify the slightest motions earlier, at around sixteen weeks or so.

Made You Look

The majority of two-timers report earlier and more noticeable Braxton-Hicks contractions, described as "warm-up" or "practice" contractions in preparation for birth. Veteran moms have reported them as early as the third or fourth months. "I never had a single contraction during my first pregnancy until the night I went into labor. With this pregnancy, however, I've felt like I've been in labor for the past two to three weeks," says Sandy, thirty-eight weeks pregnant. "My midwife says it's perfectly normal to have many more contractions prior to delivery with subsequent pregnancies, but this is ridiculous. Almost every day I go through a period when I'm wondering, could this be the start of labor?"

Indeed, Braxton-Hicks contractions can be tricky to distinguish from actual labor even if you've given birth once or twice before since they are more intense with each pregnancy. "With my second, I had a lot more trips to the hospital with false labor due to Braxton-Hicks. It was very easy to mistake them for the real thing. They would be regular until I got to the hospital. They knew my face and name by heart by the time it was the real thing," says Lauren.

Pillow Quests

Less surprising, but notable, is the increased fatigue women report with their second pregnancies. The demands of another child will likely keep you from napping, eating, and simply regrouping at all the times that you should. A firstborn's sleeping (or rather, waking) habits can also cut into your downtime. As a result, many women report feeling more tired during a subsequent pregnancy than they were with their first.

Explains Sandy, "I'm definitely more tired this time around, both because of all the contractions and because I'm chasing a toddler around. During my last pregnancy,

I was pretty bouncy right up until the day I delivered. This time, though, I'm tired, achy, and ready to get this thing outta here!"

It may be likely that your firstborn hasn't yet mastered the concept of a full night's sleep. Or even if he has, he may begin having sleep problems associated with separation anxiety or if there's increased anxiety in the household. And with a young child to tend to day and night, a job to get done, and a houseful of housework, second-timers are likely to ignore their bodies' pleas for rest. That's not wise.

Getting enough rest is as important for your baby as eating right and staying active. If you are frequently exhausted, let your practitioner know how you're feeling. And don't try to fight the fatigue: Listen to your body. It may not be a practical option, but stop what you're doing (or slow down) when it becomes hard to ignore. Go to bed a half hour earlier for a week and see if that helps. Or you may need to try a little more creative snoozing:

- If you stay at home with your child, try to nap when he naps.

- Women who work part- or full-time need to rest during lunch hours and breaks.

- Wherever you spend your days, squeeze in relaxation periods whenever possible; if sleep isn't an option, put your feet up and think calm thoughts.

- Trade child care with neighbors regularly.

- Let your spouse or partner handle baths and bedtimes more often.

Complications, Revisited

It's realistic to be concerned about first-pregnancy complications repeating themselves, particularly if the problem grounded you or gave you a good scare last pregnancy. Those who experienced preterm labor, gestational diabetes, or other major problems with a first pregnancy should expect to be carefully monitored this time.

Women who have suffered preeclampsia with first pregnancies are actually a little better off this round since, traditionally, this disease is confined to first pregnancies. Rh disease, on the other hand, is a problem that occurs almost exclusively in second or later pregnancies. A woman with Rh-negative blood doesn't build antibodies to her baby's Rh-positive blood until she's exposed to it during labor. Consequently, if the next baby is Rh-positive and the mother isn't treated, these antibodies attach to and destroy the fetus's blood cells, causing anemia or, in extreme cases, heart failure. However, injections of Rhogam given to the mother at around twenty-eight weeks— and again postpartum if necessary—can head off potential problems.

TWINS AND MORE

Expecting multiples (twins, triplets, or more) takes a toll on a pregnant body—leaving less energy for existing children and an overworked partner. What's more, both parents may also be more anxious about the physical, emotional, and financial pressures of dealing with three or more children. The following organizations and resources can offer ideas for meeting the trials and triumphs to come:

- National Organization of Mothers of Twins Clubs (PO Box 23188, Albuquerque, NM 87192-1188; 800–243–2276 or 505–275–0955; http://www.nomotc.org/;info@nomotc.org): a network of support groups for parents of twins and higher-order multiples. Call for information and referrals to local chapters.

- Mothers of Supertwins (PO Box 951, Brentwood, NY 11717; 516–434–MOST): a support network of families who have or are expecting triplets, quadruplets, or more.

- The Triplet Connection (PO Box 99571, Stockton, CA 95209; 209–474–0885; http://www.inreach.com/triplets; triplets@inreach.com): a "network of caring and sharing" for multiple-birth families offering encouragement, publications, and other resources.

- Twin Services (PO Box 10066, Berkeley, CA 94709; 510–524–0863; http://www.parentsplace.com/readroom /twins/index.html; twinservices@juno.com): offers health and parenting advice, moral support, and referrals to families expecting and/or rearing twins, triplets, and higher-order multiples.

- Twins Foundation (PO Box 6043, Providence, RI 02940–6043; 401–274–8946): This nonprofit membership organization and research information center on twins includes a national twins registry and a quarterly newsletter.

- Twins Magazine (PO Box 5350, South Rosalyn Street, Suite 400; Englewood, CO 80111; 800–328–3211; http://www.twinsmagazine.com): a bimonthly magazine that puts readers in touch with the unique world of multiples—twins, triplets, and more. Articles cover prematurity, twin parenting, health, life as a twin, and more.

Weighty Issues

Pregnant women don't leap onto their doctor's scales with wild abandon. No, given the choice, I think most would rather pee into a little cup than haul themselves up onto these humiliating contraptions to be judged by a nurse who can actually see her feet. Then there's the poor morning-sickness-wreaked soul who can't even think about an il-lustration of food, who is chided for not gaining enough.

Interestingly, a large percentage of women actually gain less with a second or subsequent pregnancy. "With my first pregnancy I gained eighty pounds, my second only nineteen, and fourteen with my third," Susan S. says. "I was only twenty with my first baby and ate a lot of junk food, hence the weight gain. So during the second I was more religious about eating well and taking vitamins. With the third I wasn't quite so zealous, but it was hard to find the time to eat anything."

Second-timers may not pack on as many pounds; how-ever, many start off at a higher weight than they did with their first pregnancies, especially when these occur within a year or two of each other. So if you find yourself preg-nant again but haven't lost all the extra poundage baby number one bestowed upon you, you shouldn't feel alone. You also shouldn't try to diet. Cutting calories at this time is a bad idea. Your body needs adequate protein for build-ing cells, calcium for strong bones and proper nerve and muscle development, a daily dose of vitamins, and plenty of energy for keeping up with the demands of other children.

In fact, you might have to make a concerted effort to eat enough during this pregnancy. Many women report feeling less ravenous than they did the first time. And even when the urge does strike, they are often on the go or busy with another child. It's not as simple to sit down for one of those midmorning snacks (like a pizza) first-timers so coveted.

Whether you're starting off way above your ideal weight or struggling to put on pounds, all pregnant women—first-timers and beyond—need to eat wisely and gain weight during pregnancy. Here are some guidelines for eating right:

- If you've got young children, you know they need to snack every few hours. Follow their lead; snack when they snack. It will keep up your energy and ward off the queasies.

- Pack nutritious foods for both you and your child in your diaper bag or backpack: nuts, dried fruits, whole-grain breads and crackers, yogurt, and peanut butter are good staples.

- Extremely overweight women can probably gain less than the recommended twenty-five to thirty-five pounds, but should be followed closely by a doctor or nutritionist.

Pregnant and Breast-feeding

Pregnancy might find you still nursing your child at a time when neither of you is leaning toward weaning. Breast-feeding during pregnancy is an option if you are extremely vigilant about your nutrient intake, particularly your consumption of protein, iron, and calcium. Understand that *both* the fetus and the nursing child will take what they can get from the mother, and if there's not enough to go around, your body will suffer. Calcium is leeched from the mother's bones if it is not supplied each day, so she must be sure to get enough in her diet and through supplementation if needed.

On the other hand, there are some situations in which breast-feeding during pregnancy may be hazardous. When a woman nurses, she raises her oxytocin levels, which can in turn bring on contractions. A woman with a history of a weak or "incompetent" uterus, preterm labor, or miscarriages may be at risk for problems. A doctor's advice is wise in these situations.

The decision to wean during pregnancy might not be up to you; about half of all children nursing during pregnancy wean themselves. Around the fourth or fifth month a woman's milk supply decreases, and some children notice a change in its taste. Toward the end of the pregnancy, the milk changes to colostrum, which may put off some toddlers. This change, plus a separation from the mother when she gives birth, may spur the child to move on. If you continue to nurse a very young baby during this pregnancy, you should consider supplementing his feedings with formula as the milk supply changes.

Whoever begins the weaning process, it's important to do so gradually and sensitively. La Leche League International suggests that you offer other kinds of loving care as substitution for breast-feeding: extra hugs, cuddles, stories, attention.

BREAST-FEEDING RESOURCES

The Womanly Art of Breastfeeding (Plume, 1997) is a classic nursing resource from the world's foremost authority on breast-feeding, La Leche League International. This breast-feeding bible addresses toddler nursing, tandem nursing, and (briefly) nursing during pregnancy. For more information, call 800-LA-LECHE to find out the name of your local LLL group leader or to request a catalog of LLL books and information.

Weaning becomes a very important issue for expectant mothers who are nursing, and *The Nursing Mother's Guide to Weaning*, by Kathleen Huggins and Linda Ziedrich (Harvard Common Press, 1994), is a good read for any woman confronting this change. Sensitive and thorough, it discusses many ways to go about it and age-by-age advice.

A New Attitude

Generally, second or subsequent pregnancies are less tense affairs than the first one. Repeat moms are apt to be less diligent about every morsel they consume (particularly when Oreos are in the immediate vicinity) and may react with less wonder about every fetal twitch and flutter. Veteran moms also own up to sipping an occasional glass of wine or savoring a cup of high-test coffee—although none are proud of it.

"I was unbelievably careful about what I ate when I was pregnant for the first time," says Rénee, mother of two and one on the way. "I wouldn't eat shellfish, bleached pasta, junk food of any kind, catsup, smoked foods, sushi. With my second I was much more relaxed—I drank a cup of coffee a day until the last month or so and I even ate chocolate. Now, pregnant with my third, I am embarrassed to say I have been craving—and eating—bacon, pastrami, and hot dogs like mad. I'm terrified this kid is going to be born smelling like a delicatessen."

Sandy admits to losing her "edge" as well. "I was definitely much more conscientious the first time. I ate really well last time, making sure I got fruits and veggies in my diet every day, and not eating too many sweets until the end. With this one, I'm lucky if I've gotten ten helpings of fruits and veggies throughout the whole pregnancy. As a matter of fact, Toll House slice-and-bake cookies have become a nighttime habit for me. I've also had a couple of glasses of wine, which I wouldn't have dreamed of doing last time. I've found you tend to pay a lot less attention to yourself when you have a toddler around."

Is it the firstborn's fault that we seek out chocolate? Not entirely. In a first pregnancy, many women allow themselves the luxury of focusing on themselves and their health for what may be the first time in their lives, and they go all out. This time they are distracted by other children, concerns about the future, job questions, and the like. They may feel as though there's less time to exercise and tend to their own health needs. And hey—are those M&Ms?

Alyson found that with each pregnancy she paid proportionately less attention to her health. "My first pregnancy, I did water aerobics and chose my foods carefully. When I got pregnant the second time, my exercise was chasing a toddler around and I wasn't as diligent about my diet. With the third, I hardly ever exercised. The only time I watched what I ate was when it was going into my mouth."

This more easygoing attitude is evident not only in a pregnant woman's meal choices but in other sectors of her day-to-day relations as well. It comes across as a hard-won confidence in her abilities as a mother, partner, and professional. She has learned to be more lenient in her expectations of herself, and more forgiving as well.

"During my first pregnancy I was working extremely hard and was very stressed at work. By the second and third I had gained more of a perspective and would say no to management if things at the office got too crazy," explains Sue B. "I guess I achieved a better sense of balance." Surely, in the delicate dance of children, home, work, and self, a little chocolate can't hurt.

As different as the children they produce, each successive pregnancy will have a personality all its own. Admittedly, that can be hard to accept when your first went by like a summer breeze and your second expectancy finds you chain-munching crackers. You'll save yourself some worry if you keep in mind that things are not "wrong" this time, only different.

Trust that your body is aware of what it needs, and will make that known. Respond to these pleas and be good to yourself.

5

The Pregnant Household

"Before Tina became pregnant again, I didn't have a lot of extra time to spend with our three-year-old son—or so I thought," Mark recalls. "But once the baby was on the way, Tina had such a rough time that she asked me to take on more activities with Chris. We had some great adventures! I actually got to know him better, and he asks for me more now. These days I can't imagine what could have been more important than being with him."

By the time a couple begins considering adding another child to their family, chances are they are running a pretty tight ship. Oh, there's occasional chaos, of course, but generally, day-to-day concerns sail smoothly along. There are routines, there are expectations, there is balance.

Anticipating a new baby, families understand that there will be accommodations, changes, refinements—but generally, they focus on the days after his arrival. In actuality, an expectant family begins to evolve months before the new bundle ever crosses the threshold. The planning, the preparing, the subtle changes in attitude and outlook that occur during second pregnancies, alter the way each family member views himself and each other.

For example, a mother may feel hindered somewhat in

her ability to manage a toddler or preschooler or by the increased fatigue a second pregnancy inflicts. Fathers may begin to feel more financial pressures and worry more about having enough time to get everything done. And children may not know quite what to make of all the excitement, but can sense that Mom and Dad are preoccupied with something. Something *big*.

This is a blessed yet challenging period. During these exciting and tumultuous months, you will all need to lean on each other for support, confidence, and love. This begins by understanding the types of issues that impact the pregnant household, and how our relationships, career decisions, and personal health become even more intertwined during this period. Hence, this chapter examines how pregnancy changes a family and how the family ultimately grows and strengthens from the pregnancy.

Roles and Responsibilities

Back to pregnancy again. Many of the first-pregnancy issues prevail; however, new concerns erupt as a family waits for baby number two. Here's what's changed this time.

Dads: More Involved, More Relaxed

Let's face it, with the majority of first pregnancies there's not a whole lot for partners to contribute. Yes, emotional support was key, as was taking on some of the housework, especially as the pregnancy progressed. And commenting every now and then about how she hardly looked pregnant or that she simply "glowed" was helpful all around.

With a second baby on the way, a partner's assistance and support are more important than ever. At a time when rest is crucial to a baby's development and an expectant mother's well-being, fathers can hold the key to a much-needed nap or a few minutes' peace that would otherwise prove quite elusive.

Unexpectedly, but not necessarily grudgingly, they may find themselves taking on more child-caring responsibilities as a second pregnancy continues. Leah Ann's husband, for instance, began planning more outings with their two-year-old daughter than he would have considered before the pregnancy, even if that meant a quick father-daughter excursion to buy some milk. "He was more willing to take Samantha with him when he ran to the store or to do other things. He also signed up for a 'tot time' class for just Sam and himself, which gave me about two hours on Mondays for me to enjoy. I've heard him say a few times to leave Mommy alone, let her sleep—that was always a pleasant surprise!"

While interested, of course, in their partner's and baby's health and development, many fathers may appear less consumed by this second round. Not that they don't care. "My husband is just as concerned with this pregnancy, but he's just not fascinated this time," says Krista. "He seemed much more interested with the first pregnancy. As a matter of fact, he told me that he sometimes forgets I'm pregnant again."

"I went to almost all the prenatal appointments, just like with the first baby, although the second time around it was somewhat less exciting," Bill admits. "I think this was due to a relative lack of novelty compared to the first time and the fact that we had a few scares (preterm labor and fifth disease) with the second. I think the scares reminded me that this parenting thing is not always lighthearted and fun."

The once overprotective, overcautious father of a first child may seem to be just a shadow of his vigilant self with number two. "I remember being about eight weeks pregnant with our first child and I had a cold," Krista continues. "On this particular day I had to go to a class, but it was raining outside and I couldn't find the umbrella. My husband actually told my mom on me because I went anyway! With this pregnancy I could be bleeding from my eyeballs and he would still expect me to perform all my wifely and motherly duties."

Well, probably not—but carrying a second child, it sure can feel that way. It's not that he loves you any less or that he is less emotionally involved in the expectancy. It's just that this time there are so many pressures in a family with children that it's easy for both father *and* mother to tune out a growing and, for now at least, quietly content fetus. Still, a kind gesture and a little extra effort around the house will mean a lot to the mother-to-be-again. Here are some ways partners can help take the load off, at least temporarily:

- Spend a Saturday alone with your child; it gives Mom some extra time to rest and will make your first feel special.

- Offer to run errands or pick up takeout on your way home from the office.

- Arrange some time alone for the two of you and surprise her with a sitter.

- Handle baths and bedtime for your older child(ren).

- Find a sport that you and your child can participate in—swimming, Little League, biking, fishing—and set aside time each week for your fix.

- Don't give up so easily. It may be harder for women to let go of some of the child-care responsibilities than it is for men to take them on—and often not worth a fight. In *The Expectant Father*, Armin Brott writes, "In all the times I've seen women plucking crying or smelly babies from their husbands' arms, I've never heard a man say, 'No, honey, I can take care of this.' " Next time, take charge.

Moms: Career Crossroads

Some women designate, more or less, a portion of their lifetimes as their "childbearing years," so that even after a first child arrives, they have a vague idea of when they would like the next one to come along. They may plan career moves or educational goals around this ideal, so in effect, this next baby doesn't derail their ambitions.

But for many women a second or subsequent pregnancy means a more drastic restructuring of their current lifestyles that goes far beyond cutting out coffee and wine. Since two children in day care can easily run over twelve thousand dollars a year, many decide to stay home with the children, at least temporarily. "I have every intention of going back to work someday," says Jeanette. "But it is cheaper for me to stay home than for us to pay a day care facility for two kids."

For women who were ambivalent about going back to work after a first pregnancy, this next installment may bring these issues back to the surface, with a vengeance. "My career objective definitely changed after having kids," explains Kayleen. "I was an elementary schoolteacher for twelve years before having my first child. I took off half the year and went back to work full-time the rest. I absolutely did not like being back at work. I wanted to be home with my one child, not taking care of thirty-three others. However, I wanted to try to continue teaching to confirm my heart's desire to stay home.

"I managed to get through the year. Child care wasn't an issue—I knew she was in good hands; they just weren't my hands. I then took a one-year leave of absence and loved being home. Over the summer I found out I was expecting our second, and that clinched our decision for me to take the year off. After daughter number two was born, I took another year off. I'm so looking forward to another year of being a stay-at-home mom. If I do go back to work, it will be part-time, at least until the kids are school age."

It's a lucky woman who finds such a happy balance.

For some, an unexpected pregnancy takes away choices and sets aside goals. "The money I was using to fund my return to college has now been rerouted to meet pregnancy and birth-related medical expenses, as well as the everyday expenses of caring for a newborn," says Sheri, who also has a twelve-year-old son. "Aside from the financial impact, the birth will also delay my return to college and completion of my degree and, in turn, the continuation of my career."

For many, second pregnancies don't require such drastic changes in professional goals, yet they spur us to reevaluate our direction to some extent. Surely some of us end up in a certain place through momentum or indecision, and a second pregnancy presents a natural opportunity to examine our desires and needs at this point in our lives. We may all question whether we are doing the "right thing" for ourselves and for our children at this time. Consider this new pregnancy an opportunity to reflect about your family and the mother you want to be.

Too Much to Do

"We daydreamed a lot more about the first baby," Elizabeth recalls. "We would relax on the couch, guessing what color her eyes would be and whether she would have a sense of humor. With our second pregnancy, I don't think we ever had time to wonder about his eye color—much less sit on the couch together."

The family doesn't shut down because one member of it happens to be carrying a fetus. There are still school plays to attend, homework to finish, play dates to plan, chores to be done, and fun to be had. And, oh yeah, jobs. This time there are fewer opportunities for singing lullabies to protruding abdomens.

It's not simply the lack of time that makes this pregnancy less of an event. As mentioned previously, spouses may seem less in awe of their expectant wife. But relatives, friends, even co-workers, tend to view a veteran mother with less reverence than a first-timer. "I remember feeling that the second pregnancy wasn't as special all around because you don't receive the same attention from anybody," says Jennifer. "Plus, you are so focused on the child you already have. Pregnant with number three, we rarely have the time to talk or dream about this little one. Sometimes I think I'm not giving my thoughts to the baby enough."

Pamela, with a third baby on the way, has found there was less help and less sympathy with each expectancy. "With the second and third pregnancies, of course my husband helped, but when there are other kids to care for, you really must rise to the occasion yourself. You just aren't as special when pregnant with number three as you were with the first. My sister is seven weeks pregnant with her first, and her husband won't even let her go to the dry cleaner for fear of chemical contamination! As a third-timer, you have to keep going and pull your weight—all of it. No time for self-indulgence."

Taking Care of Each Other

With children, a fetus, and a houseful of present and future concerns, a couple can quickly forget to set aside time to simply enjoy each other. As elusive as this notion may sound, it's an important goal to set for yourselves at this time in your lives. You both spend enough time tending to family and to work; taking breaks from day-to-day pressures is good for the pregnancy, healthy for your relationship (which can be, in turn, good for your children), and a boost for your soul.

Keep in mind that once the new baby arrives, there may be even fewer occasions to be alone. So in these precious weeks preceding a family addition, be sure to take some opportunities to rebond:

- Try to get out alone together at least once or twice a month. You don't need to schedule anything fancy— go to the drive-in, have a sunset picnic, or get to know each other again over decaf.

- Attend a marriage-encounter weekend. Contrary to popular opinion, these are not designed specifically for failing relationships, but rather for couples who hope to focus on each other away from the tensions and distractions of everyday life and to learn to improve the way they communicate with each other. These loving retreats are nondenominational; however, there are Lutheran, Baptist, and Jewish-sponsored versions, to name a few. For more information, call Worldwide Marriage Encounter at 800–795–5683.

- Take a vacation—either alone or with your firstborn. You will be amazed at how much more you can enjoy your family when you remove yourselves from deadlines—both work- and self-inflicted. This is not the time to go extreme: Choose a destination that allows for frequent rest periods and quieter pursuits. The best time to travel is in the second trimester, when the morning sickness and fatigue of the early months is done with and most pregnant women discover renewed energy. After thirty-two weeks, women should stay closer to home in case the baby makes an early appearance—remember, second labors tend to go faster.

- If you are considering taking a childbirth class this round, you may be able to locate one that incorporates a complete course into a romantic weekend away, such as Joyful Expectations (800–752–5002 or 516–754–4092) in New York or Birth Indulgence Weekends (617–784–5752), held at sumptuous hotels in Boston. These classes combine full childbirth courses with hotel accommodations, health-club privileges (ladies, avoid the hot tub), and the opportunity for a candlelit dinner just for the

two of you. After dinner, you can retire to your luxuri-
ous room and practice your breathing.

Staying Healthy

Of all a family's goals during the expectant months, the
most important during this time should be keeping your
family healthy. In these days of preoccupation, however,
well-intentioned families may find themselves heading the
other way: The morning-sick mom may have trouble preparing a well-balanced meal—or any meal, for that matter;
dads may lower their resistance to infections by working
too hard, not sleeping enough, trying to do too much.
And kids get sick—there's not much you can do about
that. But these days, childhood infections can be hazardous not only to the afflicted child but to the remainder of
the family, right down to the fetus in some cases.

Does this mean that parenting can actually be hazardous to a pregnancy? Not exactly. But there are aspects of
the job description that don't lend themselves very well
to fetal and maternal health, such as caring for sick children and carrying weary toddlers. We can't avoid these
situations completely, of course, but there are steps we
can take to minimize risks.

Two in One Year

If a woman becomes pregnant within three months of
her last delivery, her pregnancy will be classified as high-
risk, and carefully monitored throughout. Because a
brand-new mother hasn't had the time to rest and restock
her nutritional stores, a pregnancy within three months
of another increases the chances of preterm delivery and
low birth weight.

The best course in this situation is to place extra emphasis on good nutrition and make a concerted effort to rest, gain enough weight, and get early and consistent prenatal care.

Pediatric Illnesses

Kids are germy little buggers, aren't they? And when they are in school or day care environments, they are exposed to quite a variety of nasty microbes that favor little kids. Unfortunately, some of these pediatric viruses that are relatively benign for them can pose risks to the health of a pregnant mother and her unborn baby. Alert your doctor if your child is exposed to or shows symptoms of any of the following diseases:

- Chicken pox (varicella): This relatively mild although uncomfortable disease of childhood is usually severe in adults who contract it and can be harmful to the developing fetus, especially if the mother contracts it just before delivering. Keep in mind that a person is considered most contagious a few days *before* the hallmark blistering, "teardrop" rash appears up until all of the lesions are scabbed, about another week. Women who have not had the disease in childhood and are considering a pregnancy should consider vaccination for their older children (routine if they are over age one) and for themselves as well.

- Fifth disease: A mild infection (actually, erythema infectiosum or human parvovirus B19) that can cause a "slapped-cheek" rash on the face followed by a lacy pattern on the arms, trunk, and legs, fifth disease has been linked to a slightly increased risk of miscarriage in women who are infected as well as a rare form of fetal anemia. Fifth disease is very common in childhood, so chances are good that you have already built up antibodies to the virus.

- Colds and flu: Kids are great at sharing, especially

when it comes to winter colds. (At my children's day care center, these tend to start in October and peter out in May.) Caring for and cuddling them during these bouts put you at risk for infection as well. If you should come down with a virus, try to rest as much as possible. If you are vomiting or have diarrhea, make sure you replace the fluids or you might become dehydrated (which can in turn bring on labor). Consult your doctor before taking any cold medications.

Expectant women can help prevent infection by washing hands frequently, particularly after wiping a child's nose, helping them on the potty, or changing diapers. Remember to soap up hands well and rub them vigorously: The number of scrubs is more important than the amount of time spent under the water. Get your children into the hand-washing habit, too.

Giving Kids a Lift

Many expectant women wonder if it's safe to pick up their children regularly (and certainly, mothers of two under two don't have much of a choice in the matter). The answer is yes, with a few caveats. For one thing, you should always lift your child or any moderately heavy bundle correctly, with a straight back and bended knees instead of folding over at the waist. Lifting incorrectly can put undue strain and perhaps pain on the pelvis, which has already become a bit looser during the pregnancy.

Frequent lifting is not a smart option for any pregnant woman, in particular one who has experienced preterm labor, early dilation, or complications. If that's the case, instead of lifting kids up for a hug or snuggle, moms should make a habit of letting children crawl or climb up into their laps and cuddling with children on a couch or on the floor.

Around the House

Certainly one would hope that the arts and crafts materials you use with your young child are nontoxic. However, your older child may be into photography, painting, model building, or other hobbies that involve materials that might be hazardous if not used properly or under certain conditions. In fact, even cleaning products can be harmful if they are not handled with care.

To keep the entire family healthy, always check the labels on questionable products for toxicity information and warnings. Pregnant women should avoid fumes and skin contact, and wear protective gloves or masks if necessary. Make sure there is adequate ventilation, and that anyone who comes in contact with suspicious substances uses them safely.

Accepting Limitations

Pregnancy can be an elating, empowering phase of a woman's life. A baby on the way makes a woman feel vital, alive—until about 7:00 P.M., that is, when about all she really wants to do is stretch out on the couch and think about fudge. In the early weeks of pregnancy, and again in the last month or two, sleep, or anything closely resembling the state, becomes a powerful obsession.

Previous children take pregnancy "treats" like naps and quiet moments and kick them just out of reach. Very young children, in particular, present a unique set of hurdles for a pregnant parent. Toddlers and preschoolers often demand undivided attention and boundless energy—rare commodities for expectant mothers. They can't quite understand what's slowing you down, and what's more, they don't care. There's a big, bright world out there full of things to put in their mouths, and they are not about to wait around for you.

For instance, in the first few weeks that Robyn was pregnant with her second child, it was all she could do to drag herself from the bedroom to the living room couch most mornings. But once she got there, her active nine-month-old son made it his business to keep her awake, cruising the furniture, crawling at lightning speed, and climbing on top of everything he could manage, especially Robyn.

Besides the exhaustion, a sense of guilt over not being more involved with Mychal made the rigors of the first trimester even tougher. "I felt bad about it, but to keep him entertained, I would turn on the television. First we'd try PBS. When the shows ended, I would drag myself up off the floor or couch and put in a *Sesame Street* tape," she says. "He probably watched about five hours of television a day during those early weeks!"

Guilt may become a factor for all pregnant parents, no matter their child's age. Toddlers don't quite understand why you need to rest with your feet up or are too tired to take them swimming. Older children may understand the physical limitations a bit more clearly, but can still feel frustrated or disappointed that one can't do all she did before. "I felt so bad for Kyle in those last few months of my second pregnancy," says Stacy. "I was so big and uncomfortable that I just couldn't do much with him. I was glad he was attending preschool by that point."

Try not to focus on your limitations, and make the most of what you can do together. If your previous activities are prohibitive, find new ones. Explore arts and crafts stores for projects you can do at home. Plan more picnics—in your own backyard, if necessary. Or find a class activity (dance, gymnastics) that she can participate in while you observe (good for after the baby's born, as well).

Surviving Bed Rest

Most growing families find that pregnancy alters the way they interact and the time and attention that have to do so. As exciting and promising as a baby on the way may be, it clearly sets limits, creates boundaries. Yet no family understands those boundaries as much as a family affected by a bed-rest decree.

As many as 20 percent of women may find themselves ordered to bed rest during their pregnancies—a result of preterm labor, early dilation or thinning of the cervix, or pregnancy complications such as preeclampsia or placenta previa. Although there has been astounding progress in the medical technology used to help "preemies" survive, the baby who is born early faces an uphill climb. Breathing, eating, temperature regulation, and development may be hampered and may result in disabilities that can last his lifetime. Bed rest, sometimes accompanied by medication, reduces the stress on a woman's body and may help prevent premature labor and its lasting effects.

Whether this bed sentence lasts a few days or a few months, the time passes slowly and takes a toll on a family. Dads are called upon to take on the majority of household duties and child care even when they work full-time outside the home. A mom on bed rest may feel worried, frustrated, and guilty about not being able to do more for her family.

It's a disappointing time for children as well, particularly for young children who can't understand the situation. However, after a few days they will begin to realize that Mommy can't go anywhere, and will begin bringing toys to you. Children who are a bit older will appreciate the lowdown on why you are grounded: Explain clearly so that they don't think the baby is making you "sick," but that your body needs special rest and care to give baby the best start he can get in the world.

Make sure you spend time with your child each day. You can even make a game of coming up with fun ways to pass the time together. For instance, Judith has found dozens of ways to spend the days in bed with her three-year-old: "We string beads; paint with dot paints (they come in tubes with felt top, so no spills); play on the laptop; use Play-Doh; color; paint books (where the paint is in the book and she only needs water and a brush); read; cut and paste with glue—fabric, sticks, pom-poms, paper; and lots and lots and lots of stickers!"

A mom needs all the help she can get while she's on bed rest, so take people up on offers to cook, clean, transport children to day care, or run errands. This takes some of the workload off the father as well. (In some cases, health insurance may cover a few hours of aid in the house each week.)

For more advice, ideas, and strength, contact the Sidelines National Support Network, a network of support groups across the country for women with complicated pregnancies and their families. For more information or to receive a Sidelines brochure, send your requests by E-mail or snail mail to Sidelines National Support Network, PO Box 1808, Laguna Beach, CA 92652; sidelines@earthlink. net; http://home.earthlink.net/~sidelines/.

MOMS ON BED REST

Kids and required bed rest make strange bedfellows. So obeying rules can be next to impossible whether you are sentenced to be off your feet for a few months or just for a matter of days. Sidelines National Support Network suggests these activities for getting through the day with small children (tailor these ideas to your home, your children's ages, and their personalities):

- If there are infants or toddlers at home, turn the bedroom into a giant playpen: Make sure everything is child-safe, spread out the toys, and keep diapers and wipes in an accessible place.

- Read lots of stories, and have a friend get new library books weekly to keep them fresh.

- Write and illustrate your own stories.

- Play "flashlight games": Make shadows on the wall, read a book under the covers, play flashlight tag.

- Go "bed bowling" with paper cups and a small ball.

- Look for all the things in the room that are a certain color or begin with a particular letter.

- Draw letters or numbers on your child's back and have him guess what you wrote.

- Use a mirror and make funny faces.

- Play "bed fishing" with magnets on a string and paper clips.

- Play board games such as Candy Land or Uncle Wiggily.

- Jigsaw puzzles can be done on a small board or table next to the bed.

- Try "bed basketball" with rolled-up socks and a laundry basket.

- Compete at balloon volleyball.

- String Froot Loops or Cheerios to make a necklace, then eat them.

- Plant a seed and watch it grow. (Beans grow fastest.)

- Make some puppets and have a show: Paper bags and Popsicle sticks are good starters, or just use one of your child's stuffed animals.

- Make a gift for someone else.

- Write a letter to someone and wait for them to write back.

- Have a coloring contest and let your doctor, home-care helper, or partner be the judge.

- Sing all the songs you can think of, the sillier the better.

- Look through baby books or picture albums.

- Tape-record yourself or someone special reading one of your child's favorite books. (Be sure to include a signal for them to turn the pages.)

Parenting while pregnant isn't easy. A second-time mom must nurture one child, grow another, care for her romantic relationship, and pay some attention to her own needs and wants. She must attend to her family's health as well as her own. A tall order for a rounding woman.

The key to getting through these joyously challenging months is to do your best, but don't take it all too seriously. Instead, take advantage of this dynamic time to reevaluate goals and ambitions, not to criticize yourself or regret the choices you have already made. Realize that an afternoon spent simply holding hands with your child is anything but unproductive. See to your family's health and well-being, but don't obsess about every mess ("nesting" instinct excluded). Explore the promise and wonder this redefining period makes available to you, and don't forget to laugh.

6

Sibling Prep 101

"Everything I've read has told me that someone Jane's age (twenty months) really can't grasp the concept of Mommy being pregnant," Leah explains. "However, I feel as though I have to do something to prepare her. We bought a book about an older sibling getting ready for her mother to give birth and it has become a favorite. Now that my stomach is getting bigger, I've started saying stuff like, 'Mommy has a baby in her tummy,' but Jane just looks at me like I'm crazy."

Don't let a child's first reaction to the news "We're going to have a baby" carry much weight. For example, the response Esther received from her daughter Alyssa was completely underwhelming. "I told her in the car, right after I got a positive pregnancy test, that she was going to be a big sister. I'm not sure if she understood, but she calmly replied, 'I don't want to be a big sister.' So we dropped it for a couple of months."

The smallest children may smile and drool, which has no bearing on their future relationship with their sibling. Toddlers to preschoolers, depending on what they know of babies, may seem indifferent. After age four, reactions could range from sheer delight, especially if the child had been asking you for a new brother or sister, to sheer horror accompanied by crying, withdrawal, and moodiness.

The idea of a new baby in the house will have completely different implications to a young child than to you as the expectant parent. He can't understand fully how his life will change or, for that matter, how long the baby will be staying. If he's over age four or is familiar with the concept of babies (from neighbors or relatives), he may have a better understanding of their permanence and therefore may be a bit unsettled about what this means for his future.

Even if your firstborn seems okay with the pregnancy idea, he may be internalizing his worries, dealing with concerns that he may not show or verbalize. Tantrums, fussiness, aggression, and sadness are signs that he may need a few extra hugs and some focused attention during this difficult time.

As the months go by, you can help lessen the glum spells and encourage the enthusiasm by preparing your child for the changes that will transform your household. This starts with including the child in your discussions about the baby-to-be and always referring to him as "ours." By keeping the firstborn involved in all the prebaby planning and excitement, he will come to understand that this brand-new child will not take his place in the family but instead will add to the richness of it.

As the older child learns that she can take part in the prebaby preparations and festivities, she'll see that she is and will remain an important part of the family. Take, for instance, Stephanie, who, at age four, cried for two days when her mom announced she was having a baby. "I sat her down and had a mother–daughter chat. I told her I still loved her very much. Then I decided to let her be a part of it all. I told her she could come to the doctor's appointments and tests, that she could pick out all of the baby items, including bedding and blankets, all the bibs, burp rags, sleepers, blankets, pacifiers, bottles, and diapers. I also let her pick out a special stuffed animal to put by the baby while he slept. It is still in his crib today."

When Will He Understand?

A common lament among expectant parents who want to prepare the sibling-to-be is that their first child is too young to understand what's going on. It's true that under twenty-four months, a firstborn will not likely comprehend the concept of becoming a sibling. A three-year-old can tell you that she's "having a baby," but can't truly fathom what it will be like to share her parents with another human being. You may read your eager five-year-old books about babies for months before his sibling's happy arrival, but that won't guarantee that two weeks after he gets here, the older child won't calmly proclaim that the baby should be returned to the hospital, thank you very much.

Sibling preparation, then, is not as much a matter of "understanding" what a new baby will mean to the family as it is keeping him involved as the story unfolds. It is sharing the joy and excitement, the changes and the concerns, and doing what you can to give him the tools to cope. You are all going to change somewhat in the months before the baby arrives and in the years that follow. That book about becoming a sibling might not make much sense right now, but in a few months, when she knows it by heart, it might just click.

Babies Themselves

Go ahead and tell your child under eighteen months that you're going to have a new baby. Just don't expect much congratulation. He probably won't sob over the news, either. Siblings-to-be who are still babies themselves can't really understand why Mommy's tummy is getting bigger or, for that matter, may not even notice. In fact, you might as well say that you're getting a new hamster or that the Easter Bunny is coming to town. Smiles all around.

A few months later, the child may have learned that you have decided to call your abdomen Baby. "My first-born will be just under twenty-two months when the baby is born," says Sandy. "We always talk about the 'baby in Mommy's tummy,' so now he comes up to my belly and rubs it and kisses it and says 'baby.' But then other times he'll come up and crawl all over it and smack it! We also talk about the baby that's going to be sleeping in the other room, and the baby that's going to be in the car with us, but for all the talking, I seriously doubt he has any clue what that means."

Toddlers and Preschoolers

Most children in this age range express enthusiasm and anticipation about their new baby brother or sister when asked. For the most part, they don't share parents' fears about sleepless nights, missing out on quality time, the long-term effects of sibling rivalry, or how they are going to get the shopping done. Usually they'll follow the example parents set for them. If you are apprehensive or anxious every time the baby enters your conversation, your child will take your cue. But if you talk about the baby with love and excitement, he or she will think of the baby as something special indeed.

These happy feelings are easy to recognize and to share. However, at this age children have a harder time identifying fears and anxieties. This is a good time to talk about these not-so-nice emotions. Renée worked with her daughter on getting her to express her real feelings, not just the ones that were positive. "Hannah was only three, but we talked about being nervous about sharing Mom and Dad, that sort of thing. I told her it was perfectly normal and okay to be worried or angry or jealous about the new baby. I think this has served her well through the two pregnancies that followed."

A pregnancy may bring up issues for this age group that may not have come up otherwise (for several years, at least), so be prepared. Namely, a child may develop a great interest in babies, including where they come from and how they got in there in the first place.

"When we were pregnant with our second child, three-year-old Ilana started asking about how babies get into mommies' tummies and kept coming back with questions until she had it all figured out," says Sue B. "We explained as best we could, that Mommy and Daddy hug very closely, but she still didn't see how that would work. We told her that Mommy and Daddy were *naked* when we hugged, and eventually she ended the questioning.

"With our third pregnancy, our son Ari, who was around three, then asked us how the baby gets into Mommy's tummy. Ilana, almost six, was in the room and said, 'Mommy, I'll answer this,' and then calmly explained that 'Mommy and Daddy did the naked hug.' Ari just said, 'Okay,' and that was it from him."

Be truthful, but don't overload your children with more medical jargon than they need to know at this point. As Ilana illustrated, if your answers are too simple, they'll be sure to ask you more questions.

Older Siblings-to-Be

The reactions from grade-school children to the news of a new baby on the way are even harder to predict. They have a better preception of how a new family member can throw a wrench into a family's routine, and therefore can form a vivid mental image of what this new setup will be like. And that can go either way.

Sheri's son Blake, who was twelve at the time of his brother Tye's birth, was "devastated" when he heard of the pregnancy. "He teared up and asked if we *had* to have a baby in the family, insisting that he didn't want to have a brother or sister. It was a hard time. Early on, he didn't even want to talk about the baby. So we backed off and tried not to push the issue."

Even older children need to be reminded of their importance in the family and, while they may need a bit more coaxing than a preschooler, should be included in doctor's visits, baby shopping, or other prebaby planning—but not forced. All the way through, Sheri invited Blake to the obstetrician's office to hear the baby's heartbeat and to ultrasound tests to see the baby on the screen, both of which he turned down at first. As Sheri's pregnancy progressed, Blake began to soften his stance. Late in the pregnancy, he chose to participate in some of the doctor's visits (although he steadfastly declined the sibling preparation class).

As disinterested as Blake seemed, Sheri believes that deep down he began to look forward to his new role. "When we received still photos of the baby from an ultrasound, we gave him a copy to keep as his own," Sheri continues. "Just before our new son was born, I overheard Blake telling a friend, 'Look—this is a picture of my baby brother.'"

Susan S. didn't have to convince her daughter of the wonderful gift that was on the way to their home. "My thirteen-year-old practically decorated the baby's room herself. She must have folded clothes and stacked diapers ten times over. She wanted those babies maybe more than we did."

Babies Everywhere

No matter your child's age, familiarizing your child early on with the concept of babies—their looks, their needs, the way they communicate and learn—can only ease his transition to big siblinghood. Up until now, his exposure to such little people may have been limited to those in strollers at the mall or in picture books. Try incorporating babies—yours and others—into your daily lives, and the concept will be less of a mystery when your bundle finally comes home.

- Talk about the baby, and involve him in the discussion as much as possible, even if you think he's too young to understand.

- Bring your child along on prenatal visits. He may be able to hear the baby's heartbeat or see a sonogram picture, which may help the baby seem more "real" to him. (Children are usually welcome at regular visits, but you should ask first when undergoing a special procedure such as an ultrasound.)

- Expose your child to real babies as much as you can. Most children love babies anyway, so let them notice them in various environments if they don't usually get that opportunity. Point them out at the supermarket, show them pictures in parenting magazines. When you see babies, talk about their needs and abilities. For instance, explain how babies cry when they are hungry, tired, wet, or want to be held; that they don't eat food like older children or grown-ups; that they sleep a lot and need gentle handling.

- If you have the option, spend time with friends or relatives with babies so your child can look at them up close, preferably in your arms at some point. Don't be surprised if your toddler or older child yells, "My mommy!" if you pick up someone else's baby. Stand your ground and don't immediately return the infant to his or her rightful parent. Explain calmly that you are just holding the baby for a little while, and invite the child to come meet the baby or gently touch him. If you plan to breast-feed, it's especially helpful to let your child observe another baby nursing from his mother if you can.

- Give your child a "baby" of his own—a doll to diaper, feed, and love. (This goes for both boys and girls.) You can use the doll to demonstrate how to support a baby's head when holding him, how to touch him gently and not to touch his face. Don't be discouraged if your child has no interest in the doll at first; he or she may rediscover it once his sibling arrives, wanting to diaper or cuddle the doll while you hold the baby.

- Start reading books or show videos about new babies several months in advance of your due date to boost his or her understanding of what's to come, but don't force them on him. Some children may actually start requesting these books (see the list of favorites later on in this chapter), but if they seem to upset him, back off for a few weeks.

- Plan a hospital or birth-center tour with your child if possible. Often this is included in sibling preparation classes.

Share the Excitement

Particularly in the final weeks before the baby's due, your house may become a flurry of activity with decorating, painting, packing, and cooking. This can be a fun and memorable time for your youngster if she's included in the festivities. Some of the ways she can contribute:

- Invite her on shopping trips for diapers, layette items, and other baby goods.

- Let her help choose baby's going-home outfit.

- Allow her to help decorate the baby's room, make up the crib, draw pictures to display on the walls.

- If she's old enough, let her help paint the baby's room; consider a new coat for her own room as well.

- Get her suggestions for rearranging and decorating (such as where to place the crib and changing table) if she'll be sharing her room with the new baby. Try to incorporate as many of her requests as you can so that she doesn't feel displaced.

- Ask her if she would like to hand down any of her baby toys or stuffed animals, but don't demand it.

- Let him help you pack your hospital bag, and let him choose a picture of himself for you to take along.

ADOPTING A SIBLING

In a child's eyes, an adoptive baby on the way is just as exciting a prospect as one that's growing in Mommy's belly. In fact, studies have shown that children under age five don't fully understand the difference anyway. So like a child whose mother is pregnant, a child expecting an adopted sibling needs to be prepared for the changes the baby will bring and what life in those early days might be like. Most important, the older child needs to know that you will still love her as much as you do today, even after the new family member arrives.

Just as you wouldn't tell a young child too early on about a pregnancy (six months is an eternity to a pre-schooler), you don't need to prepare a child for an adoptive sibling's arrival before all arrangements have been made, particularly since this may take months or years. As soon as you do find out about the possibility, though, share this news with your first child.

If you are planning to adopt a second or subsequent child, the following resources may be of interest:

- Adoptive Families of America (3333 Highway 100 North, Minneapolis, MN 55422; 800–372–3300 or 612–535–4829; http//www.adoptivefam.org; info@ adoptivefam.org) provides support, problem-solving assistance, and information about the challenges of adoption to adoptive and prospective adoptive families. Offers publications and catalogs of helpful books and audio materials.

- National Adoption Information Clearinghouse (PO Box 1182, Washington, DC 20013–1182; 888–251–0075; 703–352–3488; http://www.calib.com/naic/; naic@calib.com) maintains the nation's most comprehensive library of materials regarding adoption and many free pamphlets and publications.

Books

- *Beginnings: How Families Come to Be,* by Virginia Kroll, illustrated by Stacey Schuett (Concept Books, 1994)

- *A Mother for Choco,* by Keiko Kasza (Paper Star, 1996)

- *Susan and Gordon Adopt a Baby,* by Judy Freudberg and Tony Geiss, illustrated by Joe Mathieu (Random House, 1992)

- *When Joel Comes Home,* by Susi Gregg Fowler, illustrated by Jim Fowler (Greenwillow, 1993)

Of Potties and Pacifiers

If you've ever moved and started a new job at the same time, you know how major life changes build upon each other to take a whopping stress toll. Same goes for young children poised to start a new preschool or master the potty while at the same time coming to terms with a new family member. Something's got to give, and bladder control is often the first to go.

Where's the Potty?

Since you can't plan your life, or your pregnancies, completely around your child's toileting habits, your best option here is to go with the flow, so to speak. If your child is making headway in the months before the baby's due date, don't back off just because regression is a possibility after the birth. There are lots of ways your child may respond to the new family member, and your child may not be as predictable as you think. Besides, the more big-kid things your child is able to handle before the baby's arrival, the better. On the other hand, don't try to rush him into training to "get it over with" before the baby arrives if he's truly not ready or interested. There will be plenty of time down the road.

If a child who has been dry all day suddenly develops frequent accidents postpartum, don't punish or scold the child for this all-too-human behavior. But don't be too quick to give up on him either. No need to hug and cuddle and reward, but don't make a big deal out of it. Slap on some new underwear and let him try again. (You're doing more laundry than usual, anyway.) If the accidents are happening during the night, try a plastic sheet under his regular bedding or, if he is a recent convert, let him wear training pants for a few days. Putting a child back into diapers, day or night, is not the best option, since you want to reinforce his abilities as a big kid.

Pleasant Dreams

Having a new sibling in the house is jarring enough without having to give up your own bed. Nevertheless, babies often precipitate a modification in an older child's sleeping arrangements, whether he has to change beds or bedrooms, or must share his own space. To minimize the resentment that might result, keep this occasion as distant from the baby's homecoming as seems practical, at least three months or so. (What's more, the first few nights after moving from a crib to a bed are not the most slumber-filled—another reason to get settled before the baby arrives, unless you want to be soothing two kids at 3:00 A.M. instead of one.)

The transition doesn't have to be upsetting, necessarily, if you present it with a positive spin. There are a lot of pluses about these changes, so be enthusiastic. Don't say things like, "The baby needs your room, so you have to move." Instead, talk about how great it will be to have a bigger room, and give her a hand in decorating it. If the child is old enough to understand about the new baby, she may want to get involved in "giving" her crib or her old room to him. Then let her pick out new pillows and bedding for her new space, and make sure her favorite stuffed animals are there to greet her.

If the baby will be bunking down in the same room as his sibling, give the child the chance to participate in its redecoration, since this "takeover" may be somewhat upsetting to him. Letting him offer his ideas about where the crib should go and what color to paint the walls will give him a sense of control. If possible, let him do some of the actual moving (say, plunking down a beanbag chair, setting down a basket).

Pacifiers, Bottles, and Other Baby Ware

Any other changes that may seem major to a young child that happen to coincide with a new baby in the house can aggravate an already delicate situation. This may not be the optimal time to take away his pacifier, wean him from bottle to cup, or attempt to keep that thumb out of his mouth. You might put the suggestions in his head—for instance, offering the cup now and then at mealtimes, or distracting him with a toy when he seems bent on finding his Binky. However, don't make a painful quest out of it. There will be plenty of time for growing up once the baby arrives. Besides, the child may have an extra need for such sources of comfort in the early days.

Siblings with Class

Nothing can take the place of a parents' preparation of a child for a new baby: the wonder in your eyes, the enthusiasm of your voice, your hugs as you describe the things a big sibling can do. As a supplement to this ongoing baby training, sibling classes offer a more objective learning experience for your child. Usually offered at hospitals, these classes reinforce what you've been telling your kids all these months, that a new baby's coming to live with you and that he's going to need a lot of love and patience once he gets here.

Children should attend a class one or two months before the mother's due date so that the ideas presented are fresh in his mind when the baby arrives. The minimum age for most sibling classes is about three, although some of the more adventurous teachers attempt to keep two-year-olds enthralled for minutes on end. Toddlers and preschoolers are often asked to bring a teddy bear or favorite doll that they will get to diaper, "feed," and swaddle. The teacher may show the children a much more lifelike baby doll and demonstrate how to hold and touch the baby. She'll talk about what they eat and how they communicate, and will probably read a book or two about new babies as well.

The instructor might also discuss all the things "big kids" can do for the new baby and to help their mommies and daddies. (Sometimes this information coming from an objective third party makes a big difference.) And if the class is given by a hospital, it might include a tour of the maternity floor and even a visit to one of the rooms. For weeks, my almost two-and-a-half-year-old couldn't stop talking about the television "way way up high" that was in a patient's room.

Classes for older kids will get more interactive, with more questions and answers and a chance to draw or create something for the babies. The teachers will delve into safety and ways that a big sibling can help around the house. Kids might get to see a slide show or a video about babies.

Susan L. decided her son, Hal, could skip the rather graphic movie on childbirth that the hospital offered to children ages six and up. "Since I was having a C-section, this was not necessary or appropriate for Hal. Instead, he and I had a discussion on how the baby comes out (the doctor cuts my belly open) and the fact that I would have lots of Band-Aids and that my belly would be very sore."

And siblings classes aren't just for siblings. Parents can learn valuable tips from simply listening to the instructor and the way she talks about the babies. The good ones will interject advice meant for the parents, initiate discussions, and provide handouts highlighting the important points. Joan recalls that her four-year-old son, Michael, was cranky and uninterested the day of his sibling class, but that she was glad they attended anyway. "We toured the maternity ward, but he didn't care. I benefited more than he did. They spoke to the mothers about what to expect. For instance, I was shocked when they said that the older child might want to try breast milk!"

The more "real" the idea of the hospital is, the less scary it will be when you are whisked away to this place. "Just being exposed to the hospital atmosphere takes some of the edge off," says Doreen Chance, who orchestrates sibling classes for Western Reserve Health Care. Even if your young child seems fairly disinterested in all of this, rest assured he's storing these experiences away to call upon later.

PREPARING FOR A STEPBABY

Announcing a new baby in a stepfamily can stir up resentments and misunderstandings if not handled delicately. Children who are living apart from a parent expecting a new baby may feel resentful or abandoned; children in the expectant household may feel confused about becoming a "half sibling." Moreover, estranged spouses may make the situation worse with negative remarks about the expectancy.

This pregnancy represents an opportunity to get some of these feelings out into the open and discuss them. If they are too difficult to express, family counseling can help. What's most important here is that feelings of hurt, anger, jealousy, or anxiety are verbalized and dealt with constructively. Let children know that these emotions are okay and that you will love them all the same. Give them the tools and the opportunity to work through these feelings, even if it gets messy for a while.

This baby might also be a first-time parenting experience for one of you. Attending a childbirth preparation class together can be particularly useful, not only to feel comfortable at the birth but to share your expectations and anxieties about the upcoming changes.

For more resources, contact:

- Stepfamily Association of America (650 J St., #205, Lincoln, NE 68503; 800–735–0329 or 402–777–7837): offers education, understanding, friendship, and support, and serves as a clearinghouse for books and educational materials of special interest to stepfamilies.

- The Stepfamily Foundation (333 West End Avenue, New York, NY 10023; 212–877–3244; 24-hour info line 212–799–STEP; http://stepfamily.org/; staff@stepfamily.org): offers support materials (articles, books, audiotapes, and videotapes) to help understand the issues and needs of stepfamily members, and counseling by phone.

Children at the Front

Some children might express interest in being present at the birth of their new siblings. Certainly this is a possibility many parents consider, if only briefly. In a hospital, young children might not even be allowed as a matter of policy. But these days, as hospitals are edging toward more family-friendly rules, your doctor or midwife might give the okay. Also, birth centers—whether freestanding or part of a bigger medical institution—are less restrictive about who attends the big event.

Three is about the earliest age to include a child at a sibling's birth. Under that, they probably won't get much out of it, and at three they are better able to understand your descriptions and express their feelings. Some researchers believe that attendance at a birth can be a positive experience for a child and influence his acceptance of the new baby. On the other hand, an unprepared or unsupervised child might find the ordeal extremely unsettling.

Ultimately the child should want to be there, but more important, he should know what to expect from start to finish. Interestingly, aspects of childbirth parents might consider "scary" are not always that way for their children. The sight of blood is often disturbing for adults but may be fascinating for a child if he's told this is a normal, natural part of giving birth. On the other hand, the sight of the mother in pain might be less traumatic for a husband who understands what is happening than for a young child who has never seen his mother so vulnerable.

Even more upsetting than the birth itself might be the inaccessibility of his parents, who must stay focused on the task at hand. That's why, across the board from hospitals to home births, it is imperative that there's a support person present for the child aside from the mother and her labor partner. The caregiver should be someone the child is already comfortable with, and he or she will make sure the child is comfortable, fed, and answer all of his

questions about the ensuing events. Like spouses or partners, children are also put at ease with ongoing dialogue
and interpretation about what's happening in the labor
room.

Because the most composed, well-prepared youngster
can become frightened or just uncomfortable during the
labor, the caregiver should leave the room with the child
whenever he asks. What's more, the laboring woman and
her partner need to stay focused on the birthing, not on
comforting. Even if the child is handling the environment
well, the mother might realize that the child's presence
inhibits her in some way. These feelings can actually slow
down labor. If this is the case, the child needs to be taken
out of the area. There's still the option of returning for
the pushing stage or immediately after the birth.

Several weeks before the birth, you can begin preparing
the child for what she might witness during labor and
delivery using pictures, videos, books, and ongoing discussions. If you have them, show photographs of the
child's own birth. Be as blunt as you find appropriate;
this is not a subtle experience. He should be aware of
what a newborn looks like; hardly the plump, smiling
baby in diaper-wipe advertisements. Also tell your child
that Mommy will experience pain and may look tired,
make strange faces, and yell or shout. Explain that these
are normal and natural.

You might also investigate sibling classes specifically
for those who might witness a birth, but they can be difficult to find. The sibling classes given at hospitals most
often teach siblings-to-be what to expect of the first few
weeks with a new baby in the house, and are not intended
for actual attendants. Check with your practitioner about
such classes. You might also track down a midwife or
childbirth educator who would be willing to meet with
your family individually.

Not all children are good candidates for birth attendance, so parents need to get beyond their particular phil-
osophical orientation and consider the child's individual
personality. In determining how a child might fare at the

birth of a sibling, temperament is much more important than how old they are. It's likely that a three-year-old could do fine at a sibling's birth, while an emotionally reactive eight-year-old might fall apart. Some children are more excitable than others, cry more easily, or overempathize with people around them. Better candidates for this level of family drama are children who recover easily from emotional upset, who can make sense of a situation quickly, and are quick to reason.

Don't let your own wishes or your idea of "a perfect birth" cloud your vision of what's best for your child. While birth is a natural occurrence, so are hurricanes, tornadoes, and earthquakes. All are awesome, humbling events to witness. The advantage here is that there is a chance to prepare for the storm.

Paint a Clear Picture

It's nice to hear about how wonderful a brother or sister will be; however, children should understand that the baby who comes home from the hospital will not be able to color, play outside, or watch videos with them. They need to be told from the outset that babies can be pretty boring at first!

But don't stress this as bad news, necessarily. On the one hand, these tiresome creatures monopolize Mommy and Daddy with almost constant demands. Not much to like there. But on the other hand, babies can't ride bikes, dance, eat ice cream cones, or swing at the park. Babies don't sit next to Mommy and Daddy at the dinner table or play in the balls at Burger King. They can't go swimming or skiing or sledding just yet.

Sure, it's nice to be carried around and get a lot of attention from friends and relatives. We'll grant the baby that much. But don't let your older child get too hung up on that idea. You can tell him that there will be visitors when the baby comes and that they will want to see the new baby. But they will also want to know what it's like to be a big sibling and will be proud of the job he's doing.

Right now your child's idea of growing up with a sibling is, at best, murky. Even a six-year-old who begs for a baby brother or sister can't really understand what she's getting herself into. Speak plainly and matter-of-factly about life with a new family member, and you may avoid a few unnecessary disappointments postpartum:

- Always refer to the baby as "ours." Make it clear that you are all welcoming him or her into the family together, and that he or she will not take the place of the first child.

- Be truthful. Don't tell your child he will have a playmate or that they will be best friends when in fact this kind of relationship will take months or years to develop.

- Don't tell your child how he or she should feel about the baby (for instance, "You're going to love being a big sister"). Maybe she will, but she can figure that out on her own. Better to tell her all the things big sisters can do and how important they are.

- Don't promise a new brother or sister specifically unless you are absolutely sure of the baby's sex.

- Help her to identify her own feelings about the baby and give her the opportunity to express her own emotions. Let her know that no matter what she's feeling, you'll always love her.

- Talk about the baby from your older child's perspective: "Will you hold the baby when it comes?" "Would you like to help Mommy give the baby a bath?"

- Emphasize the positive points about being a "big" sister, but don't rush her to grow up too soon. Be more generous with hugs and kisses—even big kids need love and affection.

A couple of months before the due date, explain to your child that Mommy (and Daddy, for a while at least) will need to go to a special place to have the baby and that Mommy may not be home for a few days. For some kids this separation is a difficult one, so several weeks' warning is a good idea (but not so early that it's a surprise again when the time comes). You can tell him that you'll talk on the phone and that he'll get to visit. Depending on your child's age, you might try a few "practice" phone calls on his play telephone.

Finally, siblings need to be made aware of what Mom's limitations will be in those first few days and weeks after the birth. For instance, they should be told that Mommy might be tired, sore, or will need to rest more than usual. If he doesn't expect this, he may think that Mommy is ignoring him or just doesn't want to play. Explain that childbirth is hard work, and that he'll be able to help Mommy by giving her lots of hugs and bringing her water or snacks.

The Final Weeks Alone

The last few weeks that your child is an "only" may seem bittersweet. You might not believe it, but you will find time to be alone with each child in the years to come—that is, if you can tear them away from each other! Resist the urge for melodrama now, and find some fun activities to share and remember:

- Do things that will be hard to do once the baby arrives, such as taking a dip at the beach or going to the movies. Dads can get more active than ninth-month moms, jumping in the colored balls or crawling through the tubes at Discovery Zone together.

- Meet Dad (or Mom) at the office for a long lunch hour together.

- Paint pictures of yourselves to hang in the baby's room.

- Gather up some pillows and comforters and stay up later watching videos. (Make it clear this is "something special.")

- Lie on a blanket under the stars and talk about the future.

Best Books for New Siblings

Here are some of the best books for exposing your child to the concepts of pregnancy, babies, and becoming a sibling. A handful of these titles are officially out of print or hard to find; however, your local library might have copies.

Babies

- *Here Come the Babies*, by Catherine and Laurence Anholt (Candlewick Press, 1993). Told in rhyme through a toddler's eyes, this is a celebration of all things baby: "Babies in boxes, babies in boots, babies on backs; Babies in socks, babies in suits, babies in packs." Happy illustrations depict the messy days and dream-filled nights of babies everywhere. Fun for all young children.

- *Mommy's in the Hospital Having a Baby*, by Maxine B. Rosenberg (Clarion, 1997). This book for preschoolers and older children centers on Mommy's stay in the hospital, using full-color photographs to explain the care she'll get, what it will be like to visit the hospital, what happens in the nursery, and what the baby will look like.

- *On the Day You Were Born*, by Debra Frasier (Harcourt Brace & Company, 1991). "On the eve of your birth, word of your coming passed from animal to animal," begins this colorful, poetic account of a child's arrival on the planet. Best appreciated by preschoolers and up, this global adventure is sure to give children a new perspective on babies and the world that welcomes them.

- *When You Were a Baby*, by Deborah Shaw Lewis and Gregg Lewis (Peachtree Publishers, 1995). A new brother- or sister-to-be may not understand that he or she was also very tiny at one time. This book explains that all people, from moms and dads to grandparents, were once small babies. Expressive photographs and simple text demonstrate babies touching, crawling, eating (messily), sleeping, learning, and growing.

New Siblings

- *Arthur's Baby*, by Marc Brown (Little, Brown & Company, 1987). Although his sister D.W. is thrilled about the new baby on the way, Arthur is less than ecstatic, giving the warnings from his friends ("You'll have to change all those dirty diapers," "You'll have to talk baby talk"). Unsure of his sibling skills, Arthur leaves most of the "babying" to D.W. But one afternoon, when no one else can calm baby Kate, Arthur proves to be a most clever and capable big brother.

- *The Baby*, by John Burningham (Candlewick Press, 1996). A sweet and simple picture book of a boy describing the new baby in his house. An enjoyable introduction for the youngest new siblings.

- *Baby Comes Home*, by Debbie Driscoll, illustrated by Barbara Samuels (Simon & Schuster, 1993). On her little sister's first day home, a sibling shares her reluctance, curiosity, and awe about her arrival.

- *Bad Baby Brother*, by Martha Weston (Clarion, 1997). Tessa is disappointed with her new baby brother, who isn't much fun, gets all the attention, and never gets in trouble. In time, though, the baby begins to respond to Tessa and she discovers the little brother she had hoped for.

- *Big Like Me*, by Anne Grossnickle Hines (Greenwillow, 1989). All the wonders and discoveries of a baby's first year are described to her through her brother's young eyes, including snow, listening to stories, squeaky toys, grass in your toes, and blowing out candles.

- *Catherine and the Lion*, by Clare Jarrett (Carolrhoda Books, 1997). Catherine wakes up, says hello to the large, smiling lion in her doorway, and tells him about her jungle gym and her new baby sister. Through heartwarming illustrations, we see Lion accompany Catherine through her busy day, comforting her as she cares for him, all the way through to her good-night: "Will you always be here?" Not a traditional new-baby title, this warmly illustrated book for all ages focuses on Catherine's courage and self-reliance.

- *Darcy and Gran Don't Like Babies*, by Jane Cutler (Scholastic, 1993). Darcy didn't like the baby, and she didn't keep her feelings a secret. Everyone told her not to feel that way, except Gran. "I never did like babies," Gran says. Together they go to the park and do lots of things only kids and grown-ups can do. On the way home they decide that it's okay to feel these feelings, and that deep down they just might like the baby after all.

- *Ellen and Penguin and the New Baby*, by Clara Vulliamy (Candlewick Press, 1996). Penguin's not sure he likes baby brothers very much—and neither is little Ellen. Until the day she soothes his cries by dancing and spinning until everyone ends up laughing together. Sweet illustrations and a touching story for young siblings through preschoolers.

- *Ginger*, by Charlotte Voake (Candlewick Press, 1997). Ginger was a lucky cat who had delicious meals and slept in a big basket. One day a pesky kitten moves in, following Ginger around, leaping onto his back, eating Ginger's food, and—you guessed it—sleeping in his basket. Ginger's just about had it, but by the end is snuggling with his new friend in a tiny cardboard box. It's a subtle approach to the new-baby theme, but the point just might get through.

- *I Wish I Was the Baby*, by DJ Long (Ideals Children's Books, 1995). A child yearns for the attention and accoutrements afforded his new baby sister, until he dreams that he's the one in the crib. He watches baby enjoying all the things he loves—playing outside, dancing, watching cartoons, eating Frooties, yet all he can do is cry, wet his pants, and get powder up his nose. In the end he realizes "she's best at being baby, and I'm best at being me." Highly recommended for kids under six.

- *Julius, the Baby of the World*, by Kevin Henkes (Mulberry Books, 1990). Lilly (a mouse) thinks her new brother's wet pink nose is slimy, his small black eyes are beady, and his sweet white fur is not so sweet. Lilly's parents, on the other hand, think that Julius is "the baby of the world." Disgusting, Lilly says. And no matter what her parents do to change her mind, Lilly persists in her disapproval of the slimy, beady baby. (You may cringe and chuckle simultaneously as Lilly works through her rivalry.) Surprisingly, when cousin Garland takes the same potshots, Lilly becomes her brother's loudest advocate. Suddenly his nose is shiny, his eyes sparkly, and his fur smells like perfume. And from then on, Julius *is* the baby of the world. In Lilly's opinion, especially.

- *Mommy's Lap,* by Ruth Horowitz, illustrated by Henri Sorensen (Lothrop Lee & Shepard, 1993). Sophie is distressed when the baby growing in Mommy's tummy takes over her mother's lap. But once Sam arrives, there is room for Sophie again.

- *My Baby Brother Has Ten Tiny Toes,* by Laura Leuck, illustrated by Clara Vulliamy (Albert Whitman & Company, 1997). A new-baby book disguised as a counting book, the little girl in this story counts up baby's eyes, hats, spoons, toys, and more. It's a fun rhyming book for all ages.

- *My Mama Needs Me,* by Mildred Pitts, illustrated by Pat Cummings (William Morrow & Company, 1984). Jason wants to help, but isn't so sure that his mother needs him anymore after she brings a new baby home.

- *A New Baby at Koko Bear's House,* by Vicki Lansky (The Book Peddlers, 1990). While most of the other books listed here attempt to affirm the negative feelings associated with a new baby in the house (and rightly so), this book takes a refreshingly positive approach to becoming a sibling. Koko enthusiastically learns about babies through books, photo albums, and visits to the hospital. When the baby comes home, she begins to cry in Koko's arms but quiets down when Mommy feeds her (you can't tell if she's nursing or bottle-feeding), and Koko feeds her dolls at the same time. This is a valuable book for parents too; each page has small-print bulleted tips for grown-ups on handling the issues each page addresses.

- *Peter's Chair,* by Ezra Jack Keats (Trophy, 1983). Peter watches his cradle and his crib get painted pink when his baby sister comes home, but is less willing to part with his chair. Gradually he realizes he is too big for these things and comes to accept his new family member.

- *Something Special*, by Nicola Moon, illustrated by Alex Ayliffe (Peachtree Publishers, 1997). Charlie needs something special to bring to his class at school. But nothing he can find is special enough, and his mom had no time to help him because she's always busy with the new baby. Feeling hurt, he peers into his sister's crib and sees a smile meant just for him. Something special indeed.

- *When the Teddy Bears Came*, by Martin Waddell, illustrated by Penny Dale (Candlewick Press, 1995). "When the new baby came to Tom's house, the teddy bears started coming," begins this reassuring book for toddlers and older listeners. When the bears start taking over the couch, it seems that there's simply no more room left for Tom. But Mom makes room on her knee so they can take turns watching the bears. Then they all take care of the baby together.

- *ZaZa's New Baby*, by Lucy Cousins (Candlewick Press, 1995). A bold, colorful, simple picture book depicting the first few days of life at home with a new baby. "My mom is going to have a baby. She has a big fat tummy. There's not much room for a hug," explains ZaZa, a little zebra about to become a big . . . well, zebra. "Dad was always busy. Mom was always busy." By the story's conclusion, however, ZaZa has some fun with baby and gets some special time with his parents. Recommended for even the youngest siblings-to-be.

7

A Birth Plan for Everyone

"I had several plans regarding who would watch Rachel when I went into labor," Mary-Austin explains. "If it happened during the late night hours, I wouldn't wake her, except if we needed to bring her to someone's house. She goes to pre-school full-time, so if the timing was right, she could stay there until I delivered. Someone in my family or one of our close friends could pick her up so that she could be the first one in the room with us and the baby. It sort of worked out that way—a good friend brought her to the hospital after school, but the baby didn't arrive until 10:29 P.M. She was almost as exhausted as I was."

The first time around, "labor preparedness" often consists of a few childbirth classes, an overnight bag packed sometime in the eighth month, and the hope that your labor partner is somewhere within your area code when transition hits. Most likely the only other being you had to consider when labor came on was your pet.

In Round Two you can't just hand your neighbor your house keys and leave your preschooler with a bowl of fresh water when the contractions start. Your childbirth considerations—such as where and how you'd like to have this baby—now must include provisions for the sibling-to-be.

You need to ensure that the child you already have gets the loving, dependable adult care he needs from the moment your labor begins through his first meeting with his new sibling.

The Family Labor Plan

If you wrote a birth plan for your first baby, it might have included directives about medications, interventions, and newborn care. This time, when you sit down to plot out your preferences, you'll need to map out a "family labor plan" that details the care of your other child or children.

This doesn't have to be as formal as it sounds, although writing it down and posting it near your telephone will help you and your partner think more clearly once the excitement of labor begins. For instance, if labor comes on suddenly, you may try calling your sitter. If she doesn't answer, call the next name on the list, and so on.

Depending on his age, including your child in the creation of the family labor plan will make him feel as though his wants and needs count, too. Ask him which friend he would like to stay with while Mommy is in the hospital or which sitter he would prefer when the time comes. Or, if it's an option, discuss the possibility of coming to the hospital or birth center and when he would like to meet the new baby. For most families, the child won't be at the birthplace, so plan to talk on the phone as soon as you can or tell him about visiting the hospital. What is most important is that you all discuss, and agree upon, your expectations and requirements for the entire labor and birth ahead of time.

Who will care for your child, and in what setting, are best decided after considering your birth options for this baby—specifically hospital, birth center, or at home.

Back to Birthing

Think back to your first birth experience. Did you use a prepared-childbirth method, and do you think it made a difference? Were you happy with the care you and your baby received? Were there things you would have done differently? No matter how many Lamaze classes you attended or how many videos you watched, a first birth is a maiden voyage, an adventure into uncharted territory. What works for some doesn't work for others, and there's no way to find out until you go through it yourself.

But second-time moms are tough. They are opinionated, educated consumers. One may have hated the episiotomy with her first birth and vowed to do everything in her power to avoid another one. Another may have held out for a natural birth with number one and has already placed an order for an epidural this round. A C-section mom may read everything she can get her hands on about VBACs (vaginal birth after cesarean) in hopes of birthing number two vaginally.

Second- (and so on) timers may snub their noses at the birthing refresher classes many hospitals offer. But don't rule it out so fast. For one thing, these don't usually take six or eight weeks (an awful lot of baby-sitting to line up): Many hospitals offer them in one day or over a weekend. And while you already know what to expect during labor, a childbirth preparation class may give you some new ideas about breathing or attitude. Says Kim, "Because the instructor for our birthing refresher course was different, I learned a few new things, which helped. Just thinking about the issues again was good—it forced me to prepare mentally a little bit more than I would have otherwise."

Some couples go back for the full course if they decide to use a new method (for instance, Bradley versus Lamaze), or if several years have passed since their last child was born. Michelle and her husband took the entire Lamaze course with both babies. "I wanted to take them with the second pregnancy because I wanted to brush up, and also because my kids were born in two different states and I wanted to see how things worked at my new hospital. So with the second we actually took the full Lamaze class again rather than just the refresher. I really enjoyed it, and I think I was much more at ease during labor."

Women having a second child may find themselves open to more options this time. "The first time around I was, I think, a little too wedded to the idea of a totally 'natural' childbirth. I felt as if it was giving in, wimping out, to use some medication. I also feared its effects on the baby," explains Amy. "The second time, I had discovered that there is no real virtue in suffering pain unnecessarily, and a stressed-out, exhausted mom is more dangerous to a baby than some mild, well-researched pain medication. I found I was more willing the second time, when back labor hit, to say I needed relief. I knew I needed help in order to keep control and work with my labor, rather than losing it altogether. That, I think, is the key point—when the pain becomes overwhelming, swamping, it's time to get help." Amy asked for an epidural but agreed to try Demerol first, which helped so much she passed on the epidural after all.

When considering new ways to cope during labor, this is also a good chance to evaluate the setting for your impending birth. There are a variety of options concerning facilities, medications, practitioners, and other points these days, and you should choose the environment that seems right for you and your family.

Hospital Births

Most women labor and deliver in hospitals, and for the most part, they are happy with this decision. Hospitals have the experience and the technology to ensure the safest welcome for a new baby and can react instantaneously if there are any severe problems during labor, delivery, or in the first few hours after birth. Clearly, in situations in which timing means everything, being at the hospital can make the difference between a healthy mother and baby, and a lifetime of problems and disability—or even death.

It's not unusual, though, for families to feel some discouragement about their hospital birth experiences. Of those women who find fault with their previous hospital-based births, a common complaint is that they lost whatever sense of control they might have hoped for at the outset. Perhaps they felt nervous or intimidated by high-tech instruments. Maybe the doctor wasn't around as much as expected, or those who didn't want pain medications felt that they were pushed rather than offered. Sometimes even nonmedical postpartum requests such as not giving the new baby a bottle or pacifier are ignored or contradicted.

This time there's no excuse not to ask for what you want. An increasing number of hospitals are instituting policies that can make labor and delivery a more personal experience. For one thing, many are creating wings with LDRP (labor-delivery-recovery-postpartum) rooms, reflecting a more family-friendly philosophy. Increasingly, traditional obstetrics practices are bringing certified nurse-midwives (CNMs) on board. So with epidurals and fetal monitors a heartbeat away, it is still possible to have a CNM deliver your baby and to keep your baby with you at all times.

Birth Centers

Some hospitals have opened low-tech facilities on their grounds dedicated to the prenatal care and childbirth needs of low-risk pregnant women. A step away from that are over a hundred freestanding (nonhospital) birth centers in the country that offer safe, attentive, welcoming settings for low-risk deliveries where women can labor at their own pace surrounded by the people they choose.

Birth centers are more like cozy inns—or rather, BB&Bs

(bed-birth-and-breakfasts)—than any type of medical facility. There are usually only a handful of rooms, filled with quilts, wood furniture, and rocking chairs; hidden from view are oxygen and other equipment for labor, birth, and the postpartum period. There is frequently some sort of family or play room with books, toys, or a VCR.

Unlike the majority of hospitals (although the tides are shifting), birth centers let you decide who will be present at your child's birth—other children, friends, family members. "It's common for women to have their own mothers by their sides," explains Susan Stapleton, president of the National Association of Childbearing Centers, the country's most comprehensive resource on these facilities. "Almost all of these mothers were robbed of the full childbirth experience—given general anesthesia, separated from their babies, and discouraged from breast-feeding. Their reactions to these births can be quite touching. And there are generations of grandfathers who never saw any of their own children being born."

Children who are to be present in any birth setting—hospital, birth center, or home—should be exposed to the birth experience through books, videos, and photographs prior to the event. In addition, they need to have a designated caregiver, not the father or labor partner, available to them at all times. (For more children attending a sibling's birth, see "Children at the Front" in Chapter 6.)

Water is the birth centers' preferred method of pain relief. Epidurals aren't allowed because of the risks involved (although some medications are available), so if there aren't Jacuzzis on the premises, a soaking tub is practically guaranteed. So soothing is the warm water, in fact, that water births are popular at these centers—sometimes planned, sometimes not. Many families go home between four and eight hours after the birth.

While hospitals are still the safest place to have your baby, the National Birth Center Study, as reported in *The New England Journal of Medicine* in 1989, revealed licensed, accredited birth centers to be safe, cost-saving, and extremely satisfying alternatives to hospital deliveries. That's due mostly to the thorough, ongoing screening process ensuring that only women with low-risk pregnancies meeting certain health criteria are allowed to give birth at these centers. (For instance, women carrying multiples and those with chronic high blood pressure, kidney disease, or diabetes would not be able to use a birth center.) This may help to explain why C-section rates for birth centers are lower than the national average (4.4 percent, compared to at least 25 percent of all in-hospital births). And in the event of a complication, laboring women can be quickly transferred if needed; all birth centers have physician backup and are affiliated with at least one hospital. Often the nurse-midwives have hospital privileges and can continue to care for their patients after they've been moved.

With such an impressive record, birth centers have won over a good many insurance companies. They will cheerfully cover birth-center deliveries, as they cost about half of what comparable hospital births might run.

Labor Doulas

Labor doulas are quite helpful for the first-time laboring woman, who has no idea what to really expect. But for second-timers, the assistance of a doula can make labor a completely new experience. The concept of the doula (Greek for "woman serving woman"), who offers continuous emotional and physical support during labor and delivery, is thousands of years old. Edged out of the birthing room by modern technology, this age-old form of labor support has enjoyed a recent resurgence as women opt for more natural labor conditions. Families and the medical community alike have taken notice of what the doula has to offer: cesarean rates reduced by up to 50 percent, labor time shortened by 25 percent, and decreased need for inductions, pain medications, and the forceps when a doula is by a laboring woman's side.

Doulas are nonmedical assistants who do not take the place of doctors or midwives and handle no clinical tasks. For the most part, doulas accompany their clients to hospitals or birthing centers and share the labor room with the parents and medical personnel. She complements the birthing team, attending to a woman's emotional needs and physical comfort with encouraging words, soothing massage, hand-holding, and relaxation techniques.

Home Birthing

For those who choose to give birth at home, the comfort of things familiar and of having family close by both relax and energize them for labor. At home, some women feel less inhibited and eager to try different labor positions and locations. Explains Kelsey, "I loved being in my own surroundings, with my own smells and my own bathroom. I was able to walk through the house and plop down whenever I felt like it and give birth. I was able to bathe with my baby afterwards, shower, get into my own clothes, and crawl into my own bed with my tiny newborn. It's not right for everyone, but it was the perfect choice for me."

A very small percentage of medical doctors perform home births; these are usually attended by midwives of varying degrees of training. A CNM has a nursing degree and is better trained to handle medical emergencies than a "lay midwife," and in some states is the only attendant of the two who is allowed to participate. Legalities regarding who can perform home births and what type of education is involved vary widely state to state; contact the organizations listed in the sidebar "Birthing Resources" for specifics about your town.

Throughout pregnancy, women might see their midwives in their homes or in the midwives' office. As with birth centers, women are regularly screened for problems that might pose a safety issue. Once labor begins, midwives are trained to recognize signs of complications and will arrange for transport to a hospital if the health of the mother or baby is at stake.

In capable hands and with backup available in the case of a complication, home births can be a safe option for low-risk, normal labors. It's imperative, though, that whatever a woman's feelings about hospitals and medical intervention, she be realistic about situations that are out of the midwives' hands. In other words, don't let your idea of the "perfect birth" get in the way of your own or your new baby's health.

Wherever she may choose to have her second baby, a woman's ultimate happiness with the experience relies heavily on the footwork she did before the first contraction hit. Create a birth plan, discuss it with your doctor or midwife, and find a birthplace that shares your vision. Knowing your wants, and making them known, will increase your chances for having your baby your way—this time.

BIRTHING RESOURCES

- American Society for Psychoprophylaxis in Obstetrics (ASPO/Lamaze; 1200 19th Street NW, Suite 300, Washington, DC 20036; 800-368-4404; http://www.lamaze-childbirth.com/; aspo@sba.com): Lamaze techniques—breathing, relaxation, understanding options—are used to help women work with, rather than against, the normal childbirth process. Contact for details and to find local instructors.

- American College of Nurse-Midwives (818 Connecticut Avenue NW, Suite 900, Washington, DC 20006; 202-728-9860; http://www.midwife.org; info@acnm.org): offers midwifery resources and referrals to local practitioners.

- Association of Labor Assistants and Childbirth Educators (PO Box 382724, Cambridge, MA 02238; 617-441-2500; http://www.alace.org; alacehq@aol.com): can refer you to professional labor assistants (nonmedical birth companions such as doulas) who accompany and support women in any birthing environment.

- The Bradley Method (or American Academy of Husband-Coached Childbirth; PO Box 5224, Sherman Oaks, CA 91413-5224; 800-4A-BIRTH; http://www. bradleybirth.com): This childbirth method utilizes relaxation and deep breathing techniques. Call or write to learn about Bradley workshops in your area, or to receive a national directory of Bradley teachers or an educational video catalog. (See also the "unofficial Bradley FAQ" at http://www.fensende.com/Users/swnymph/Bradley1.html.)

- Cesareans/Support Education and Concern (22 Forest Road, Framingham, MA 01701): provides emotional support for cesarean delivery families; distributes information and promotes education on cesarean childbirth, cesarean prevention, and VBAC (vaginal birth after cesarean); and hopes to influence attitudes and policies that affect the cesarean childbirth experience. Send a self-addressed stamped business-size envelope for a brochure and a list of C/SEC publications and other resources.

- Doulas of North America (1100 23rd Avenue East, Seattle, WA 98112; 206-324-5440; http://www.dona.com; askdona@aol.com): offers information about and referrals to labor doulas.

- Informed Homebirth/Informed Birth and Parenting (PO Box 3675, Ann Arbor, MI 48106; 313-662-6857): IH/IBP presents parents with information on alternatives in birth and parenting, as well as resources, books, and videos on home birth and referrals to childbirth educators, birth assistants, midwives, and midwifery training.

- International Childbirth Education Association (PO Box 20048, Minneapolis, MN 55420; 800-624-4934 or 612-854-8660): ICEA has publications and information on "family-centered maternity care," childbirth alternatives, and breast-feeding.

- Midwives' Alliance of North America (PO Box 175, Newton, KS 67114; 316-283-4543; http//www.mana.org): provides free brochures and referrals for expectant parents.

- National Association of Childbearing Centers (3123 Gottschall Road, Perkiomenville, PA 18074-9546; 215-234-8068; http://www.birthcenters.org; birthctr@midwives.org): The country's most comprehensive resource on freestanding birth centers, NACC offers referrals to local licensed and accredited birth centers, as well as guidelines on selecting a birth center, for a $1 donation to NACC.

Built for Speed

While second labors don't necessarily commence any earlier—or hurt any less—on average, they are faster and more efficient thanks to a seasoned body and mind. According to a study conducted by the University of New Mexico College of Nursing, the mean length of active and second-stage labor (from four centimeters dilation to birth) was six hours, compared to nine hours for first deliveries. Physically, a body that's been there before has been primed: The cervix may efface and dilate with fewer contractions after having been stretched to ten centimeters in the past. The elasticity of the cervix shortens the pushing stage to an average of twenty minutes (down from an hour in first pregnancies), and decreases the need for episiotomies.

And psychologically speaking, women may "get into" labor more easily and with less anxiety. The benefit of experience tends to give women more of a feeling of control then they felt in previous labors. Knowing what's in store, they tend to be more relaxed about the entire event, and are more able to focus on birthing naturally.

"What a difference in labors!" says Michelle. "My first labor started in the wee hours of the morning, and lasted nine hours. With my second labor, I had mild contractions for a couple of hours that I thought were Braxton-Hicks. The next day at a routine appointment I was told I was already four centimeters dilated and ninety percent effaced! The active labor, once my water was broken, lasted an hour and fifteen minutes!"

In Robin's experience, the second labor was also faster and easier. "The birth of my first daughter took fifteen hours *after* my water broke naturally and was excruciatingly painful the whole time. The birth of my second daughter was less than two hours from the time my water broke, and the pain never got above a seven on a scale of ten."

Remember, though, that faster doesn't necessarily mean easier. The active labor and pushing stages are statistically shorter, but there are no guarantees about the hours or days leading up to that. For instance, it's not unheard of for a second baby to inflict days of back labor or to fake you out with a couple of false starts.

And as Sue B. found out, the shorter-labor rule doesn't apply to everyone. "My labors and deliveries were all very different than what I expected. Ilana's, our firstborn, was the shortest—less than twelve hours. I had wanted to do most of my labor at home, which we did. What threw me off was that the doctor told us to wait until the contractions were five minutes apart and regular. That never happened to me. They would be three minutes, then eight minutes. So by the time we went to the hospital, I was ten centimeters dilated and ready to push. Ilana was born an hour later.

"With Ari, our second, I was paranoid about getting to

the hospital earlier. As it turned out, labor with Ari just dragged on and on. We finally went to the hospital after four nights of contractions. The contractions were still not very strong or frequent, and we were nervous. Plus, the doctor had me start pushing at nine centimeters, but I think that was too early. The contractions slowed down and were about nine minutes apart. Pushing for two and a half hours wiped me out both physically and emotionally. Finally the doctor said to stop pushing and consider Pitocin. I don't know if it was taking a rest or the mere threat of the Pitocin, but fifteen minutes later Ari came out."

Whatever happens with number two—a shorter, intense labor; a longer, more complicated affair; or a second C-section—it may be somewhat easier to bear. This time you know that you can get through it, that it will end eventually, and, most of all, what's waiting for you once the work is over.

Labor Day Child Care

Assuming you plan to give birth in a hospital or birth center, you may have to leave home for a day or more before your child even gets to visit with you. This can be especially hard on a young child who hasn't been separated from his parents for long periods. The best thing you can do for your child is to make sure he understands why you have to leave, where you'll be, and when you will be coming home, and try to arrange a plan that maintains his usual routine as closely as possible. If he usually goes to day care or to school, try to get him there. Don't let him miss any after-school activities or favorite play groups if you can arrange it.

"Since we live in a town about forty-five minutes away from the big-city hospital where I was to deliver, we had several friends lined up to see after Blake, pick him up from school, get him to baseball practice—whatever his immediate needs were," says Sheri, whose son was twelve when baby brother Tye was born. "We felt it was important, in light of his ambivalence about the baby, that we not allow the birth to disrupt school, sports, and other activities that were important to him. As it worked out, Blake had a full schedule of activities planned when I gave birth, so he was with friends throughout much of the day and then spent the night with another family."

In a best-case scenario, especially when younger children are involved, a caregiver will come to your house, so that the child can play with his own toys and books and sleep in a familiar bed. The hard part is finding someone with whom your child is already comfortable who can pull this off. When considering caregiving candidates for the big event, keep in mind these trustworthy possibilities:

- Your first thought may be your child's usual babysitter. This is a great option since your child is already familiar with him or her. It's not so great if the sitter has an early curfew, though: You may need someone to stay with your child at least twelve hours in a row or more. Is the sitter up for these extended hours?

- Relatives are also good candidates for this role, but proximity is often a problem, especially for today's widespread families. If this route seems right for your family, perhaps a sitter or neighbor could step in for a few hours while your parents, siblings, in-laws, or cousins are in transit.

- Neighbors and family friends are key candidates, especially for late-night emergencies. Those within walking distance or on the hospital route get a gold star.

- Day care center teachers are another possibility, although sometimes center policies forbid this. If this sounds like an option, have the teacher visit your house once or twice or take your child to hers if that would be the more likely scenario.

• If you participate in a play group or mother's club, you may find someone in one of these communities who can step in when the time comes. Put the word out at your next gathering and you will probably be flooded with offers. If you don't attend a play group or mothers' group, now may be the perfect time to join one. Inquire at your child's preschool or day care center or your pediatrician's office, or check the local newspaper.

If your child will need to stay with a friend or relative, consider packing a bag ahead of time for his trip, just as you would for your hospital stay. You might want to make a note on your family labor plan for items for your child's to grab at the last minute: a special teddy bear, book, or blanket that he would miss if they were packed away for a few days beforehand.

Your family labor plan should include detailed instructions for whoever will be caring for your child regarding meals, bedtime rituals, toileting, and favorite videos or games. These details may escape you if the new baby decides to make a somewhat dramatic entrance (early, quickly, painfully). Moreover, this plan should discuss when you would like your child to meet the new baby. The caregiver needs to know this, since some parents want to get their kids together as soon as possible. For example, you might put in a call to your caregiver when pushing begins or immediately after the birth so that they can get on their way.

Have a Backup Plan . . . or Three

Whomever you choose to care for your first child while you're giving birth to your second, you'll need to think through and rethink your plan thoroughly. People's lives go on whether your baby arrives three weeks early or two weeks late, and no one can guarantee that he or she will be available for you and your child around the clock, whatever the weather, for over a month.

Since second and subsequent labors tend to go faster than the first, you may have no time to waste once the baby begins his journey. Our neighbors discovered this when, eleven days before her second child's due date, Sarai sent her visiting mother home a few hours too soon. I had often suggested to Sarai that we would be happy to care for Alexandra, then almost two, when the time came. But Sarai seemed confident that her mother would be able to make the three-hour drive from her home in time to tend to their daughter once labor began.

The plan might have worked if Sarai's mother hadn't been on the road in the wrong direction when the first contraction hit. What's more, Sarai paid little attention to the increasing intensity of the contractions since she still had almost two weeks till her due date.

At 8:00 P.M. I received a call from Sarai, who could barely speak an entire sentence without gasping. She asked if we could watch Alexandra until her mother arrived—seems they had left a message on her answering machine that she should turn around and head back. We said we'd love to. At 8:30 Sarai's husband, Craige, showed up breathless and beaming on our doorstep, holding a bewildered toddler and an assortment of clothes and books tossed into a bag. Less than forty-five minutes later Sarai called me from the hospital to tell me she was holding her new little boy!

Our neighbors taught me some valuable and somewhat frightening lessons that night, considering I was five months pregnant at the time and had a sleeping toddler upstairs myself. I learned that (1) a second-time mother should take all contractions seriously and (2) I needed a list of possible caregivers for every situation and scenario that could possibly occur.

When writing this section of your family labor plan, be

as brutally honest with yourself as possible. Imagine worst-case situations, no matter how scary: preterm labor, an out-of-town spouse, or a middle-of-the-night emergency. Leave nothing to chance. And remember that you will probably need different plans depending on the time of day and the day of the week. Get home and office telephone numbers from any potential caregivers, and make a note of whether they have access to their own transportation.

Beepers are often available from hospitals, or check your local telephone book. Sometimes you can get several at a discounted rate. You may want to give these out to whoever is on your list a few weeks ahead of your due date.

Second-Time Dads

Just as moms may be more relaxed and confident about the second labor and delivery, most dads are more at ease with the birth process and their role as support person. "He was much more relaxed about the second birth," explains Sheri. "Both times he was very actively involved; in fact, too involved the first time, insisting on telling *me* when the contractions were coming! This time he was much calmer, which, in turn, helped me relax."

"The second labor was much more enjoyable for Gary," says Leah Ann. "The first was very hard and the C-section threw him out of the loop. With this baby, he was there for every 'icky' detail. He seemed to be more at ease with this one—he cut the cord and held the baby first. It was perfect and he still talks about it today."

Some women are taken aback when their partners seem a bit too relaxed for their tastes, as Pamela describes: "During the second birth, he was much more casual. I will never forget him eating my lunch, which I wasn't allowed to have, watching TV in the labor room while

I'm in labor saying 'I'm going to throw up! I'm going to throw up!' He calmly held the basin for me, then went back to finish my lunch."

"The first time I had Ed's complete, undivided attention and he was absolutely amazing," Renée explains. "The second time he dared to lie down and fall asleep while I was making my way from six to eight centimeters without drugs! Needless to say, I had a minor fit because it unexpectedly hurt quite a bit—the second baby weighed a full pound more and was in a bad position. I wouldn't say Ed was completely jaded, though. Admittedly, he was a little too casual about the whole labor thing the second time around, but I am happy to report that when the baby popped out, he was crying every bit as hard as he was when our first made her entrance."

The First Meeting

The siblings' first meeting may seem a pivotal moment, or at least a Kodak one. It is an important milestone for your family, but their interactions are not as important to their future as family members as you might expect. At the very least, a pleasant experience for the older child may help him bond with the new baby sooner.

As soon as it's feasible, Mom should telephone the older child and invite him to come visit and meet the baby. When he arrives, she should have free arms for lots of hugs and reassurance. Don't force the new baby upon him; let him warm up to his sibling at his own pace. There will be plenty of time for kissing and holding the baby. If he seems more interested in the TV or the sink, humor him and let it go at that.

It shouldn't come as a surprise that children under eighteen months might not make much of the new arrival. Jeanette's son Ben was only thirteen months old when brother Cody arrived. When he came to visit the next day, "he hated the hospital and wanted no part of the new skinny me," she says. "He was not impressed with his new brother at all."

A lot of kids, though, are passionately interested in "their baby," at least at first. Says Aimee, "Lyxi (two and a half) was so excited that it was a girl, she was ready to play! She held her right away and flooded her with kisses. Every time someone else would take baby Madison, Lyxi would say, 'No, she's *my* sister! I need to hold her!' She rocked her and sang songs to her. It was so sweet it brought tears to my eyes. She didn't want to leave when it was time for her to go home, she just wanted to be with her sister."

Older children might display a more complex reaction to their sibling, so be prepared. Five-year-old Stephanie met baby Joshua within minutes of his birth. And while these initial moments bordered on the magical—"she helped give Joshua his first bath and held him before he was an hour old"—Stephanie had a rough time later that night. "The night Joshua was born, Stephanie really acted up with all the people coming to my room," Connie explains. "My nieces wanted to sit by me to see the baby, so Stephanie went tearing out of the room crying. She wanted the baby for herself and no one else. This continued for about an hour and she hid in the bathroom the whole time. I just let her be, kept telling her I loved her. My sister-in-law took Steph down to the gift shop, and when they returned, Stephanie handed me a card and a flower. She also gave me a big hug and said she was sorry. After that, all the kids were on my bed with me and the baby."

The first meeting might have to be postponed if there are any complications during the delivery—frustrating for a newly promoted sibling but worth the wait. "The baby had a few problems that necessitated a stay in the neonatal intensive care unit that first night," Mary-Austin continues. "So Rachel didn't get to see the baby until the next afternoon. At the time she was so excited and immediately wanted to hold him, which she did like a pro!"

Obviously you can't force this first meeting to go one way or another, but following these general guidelines might make it a more positive experience for everyone involved:

- Limit the number of other people in the room during the child's first visit. Just you and the new baby are overwhelming enough.

- Don't tell the child how to feel or what he should think. Back off and let things happen.

- An exchange of presents (a "big sibling gift") is a nice way for the older child to reach out to the new baby, and it reassures him that his new role is exciting and important as well. Good presents for the baby: bath sponges, hooded towels, a soft toy. Presents from baby to sibling (depending on age): stickers, markers, videos, accessories, or a favorite CD.

- Let your child set the pace for the meeting. Don't force him to hug, kiss, or hold the baby. If he asks to do these things, explain the right way to do them and help him if needed.

- Let him leave when he's ready. And don't let him exit without a hug and a kiss, even if he was monstrous throughout the entire visit!

PART THREE

Your
New
Family

When you left for the hospital, your family thought they knew each other pretty well. Now, home with a new baby, you've got your doubts. Your preschooler is doing things he's never done before (or things he hasn't done since toddlerhood). You barely recognize your body and are sobbing at the drop of a hat. And you think you remember your husband, but you don't really see him awake enough to be sure.

These days of exhaustion and confusion will improve quickly as you begin to find your way and carve out a routine. Your firstborn may test the limits of your love daily, but you will always pass. You will discover new ways to get things done and innovative solutions to a new crop of big-family problems. Eventually you will be able to feed, dress, bathe, and step out with your children (and a large diaper bag) on your arms, and you will hold your head high.

Welcome home! This is the beginning of a beautiful family.

8

Coming Home

"Isn't he cute?" Maria asked her daughter, holding her swaddled newborn son for her three-year-old to see and touch. "Yes," the little girl replied. "Who's going to be his mommy?"

During my pregnancy with my second child, I remember that I wasn't all that nervous about the impending labor— hey, that was going to *end*. I was more concerned about what we would all do with each other once we got home. Would my daughter truly grasp that this new baby was here to stay? For that matter, would I? And since he was going to be with us for quite some time, how could we possibly keep *two* children feeling happy, fed, clean, and loved? Would there ever be time left over for ourselves? And what was our dog's name again?

No one can tell you what those first six weeks are going to be like and how you will get through them, but I'd bet my dog what's-his-name that you will survive it. You have already been through the new-baby routine once before, so you're no stranger to postpartum parenting. The more dubious variable will be your firstborn. She may embark on a test of your patience and love so exacting that you may come to question it yourself. She will ask for the world and then push you away when you deliver it.

Now put aside everything you have been thinking about what your new life with two kids will be like and come on in.

Expect the Unexpected

The first thing about having two children that caught me off guard was how enormous my toddler appeared once I got my hands on my new baby. Sara towered over Joshua, dwarfing him in her shadow. Simply picking her up—as she requested several dozen times each day—became a herculean undertaking. As I held her in my arms, her legs dangling down to my knees, she seemed almost as tall as I was. How could she have grown so much without my noticing?

This was just the beginning of a host of changes in my perceptions. Bring a new baby home and it is as if all the physical laws of the world as you know it are on holiday. Day is night, night is day. Clocks actually move more slowly when the baby is awake, and speed up when he's asleep. Basically, you shouldn't count on anything to go the way you want it to or how you think it might.

For instance, you might have been confident in your ability to comfort your older child, care for a new baby, and recover from childbirth with some assistance from your spouse or partner. This can go either way. Sleep deprivation, one of the nastier side effects of parenting, hits you harder when your other child develops sleep disturbances as well, and may hinder your ability to soothe effectively. Well-meaning, well-rested friends may advise, "Sleep when your baby sleeps," but unfortunately newborns tend to sleep only when a sibling is awake. (They want you all to themselves.)

And if you think you can predict how your child will

handle it, well, you'll find out the truth soon enough. Whether you think your child will be shattered by a new baby or will take it in stride, you won't know until you all spend at least twenty-four hours in the same dwelling. Understandably, children are at their unpredictable best when a new baby finds his way into their homes.

My advice: Stay flexible, and stay sane. Setting your goals too high in the first week will almost assuredly send you straight into a postpartum funk, whereas putting your expectations on hold for a while leaves plenty of room for error. Let your family flow, find its meter, take its new shape.

"Second" Nature

The upside of bringing home a second baby is that all those things that seemed so foreign with the first—breast-feeding, diapering, even dressing the kid—are almost second nature in comparison. The day Sara had her first sponge bath at home, I recall, my husband and I spent twenty minutes arranging all of our "tools" and another thirty cleansing her with a progression of cotton balls, alcohol wipes, and washcloths. For that matter, we both assisted in her bath for several weeks, as if one of us had to be there in case the other required more baby shampoo or dropped a towel. But when Josh came along, I didn't have an hour to spend wiping and dabbing—he was a seven-pound baby; how much skin did he have, anyway? And my husband has yet to assist me.

With number two, there's less of a learning curve regarding baby-care basics. Parents are already familiar with diapering and burping and can swaddle with the best of them. They are also better prepared for sleepless nights than they probably were with their first. Says Larry, "It was much easier getting back into the baby routine with the second than it was trying to adjust to the first one. This time we were both better able to anticipate his needs and react accordingly."

The presence of an older child may take some of the edge off the bevy of new-parent anxieties. "I think I was more confident when our second daughter, Anne, came home," Bill explains. "But I think a lot of that had to do with having another kid around to worry about. I couldn't fixate on trivial things about the new baby."

Recovering may be easier and quicker for a woman who has been through childbirth before, although "afterpains," powerful contractions of the uterus, may seem more intense with each pregnancy. (Your doctor may suggest prescription-strength ibuprofen or the like.) She knows what works best for her body and what will put her flat on her back again. Susan L. had both of her children by C-section, and was out of bed sooner with the second because of her experiences with the first and subsequent abdominal surgeries. "I learned that the faster you force yourself to start moving around, the faster the overall recovery was. So for the second C-section, I was out of bed much quicker. I was back in the office picking up mail after ten days—even I couldn't believe how good I felt."

"YOU GOTTA SEE THE BABY!"

Everyone loves babies—and they are all coming to your house to take a look. That's fine, if you are feeling up to it. But keep in mind that all too often visitors tend to forget that there's another child in the house who, incidentally, was there first. Show off your newborn, but stand by your older child by following these suggestions:

- Limit visitors to the house, particularly the first day or two after the baby comes home. Your child needs all the attention you can spare in these early days more than interested neighbors or extended family members. Discourage "drop-ins."

- It's thoughtful for visitors to bring a present for your first child when they bring something for the baby, but it shouldn't be expected. You should prepare your own stash of gifts to have at the ready to soothe their souls. (Simple is fine: stickers, crayons, small stuffed toys, a baseball.)

- Remind visitors to pay some attention to the older child, or at least nudge them in that direction by incorporating the child into conversations. "Yes, the baby is sweet. And Julia is enjoying being a big sister to him. Julia, can you tell Aunt Mary how you've been taking care of the baby?"

- If anyone should ask what you need, or if you find yourself a visitor in someone else's new-baby household, remember the gift of food. Any prepared meals, gift certificates, or prepaid delivery services will be hungrily appreciated.

Go on with Your Life

The secret to getting through the first weeks as a "mob" is to *modify* your routine. Note, I am not saying "abandon all sense of routine," because if you do that, you will find yourself unshowered and still in your pajamas at two in the afternoon with a poorly rested, hungry preschooler on your hands. By definition, routines are habitual, unimaginative, rote procedures, and if there's one thing you need to make your new family work, it's creativity.

- Find ways to maintain a sense of order by adjusting your new baby's needs to the workings of the family. For instance, feed older children decent meals at nor-

mal intervals or risk setting off their fussy alarms;
baby can cry a few minutes while you get things set
up. Only in rare cases should personal hygiene be
optional.

• Enlist help from friends, neighbors, other parents, but
find *some* way to get them to their day care, play
groups, or gymnastics classes. Bring baby along if
necessary.

• Toddlers in particular need to know they can expect
the expected, but adjust the expected accordingly. If
your toddler is used to bath, brushing, and books at
bedtime, don't let the new family member dictate otherwise. On baby's particularly fussy nights when the
divide-and-conquer technique is not an option, the
bath might be a bit shorter than usual or there might
be less time to savor every illustration. You could always promise an extra book for the next evening.

• Make the most of the wee hours. Until the baby figures out the difference between night and day, there
are going to be at least a few weeks of late night
snacking. But don't despair—enjoy these chances to
spend time alone with the new guy. "I loved nursing
my son during the night," a nurse told me. "It was
the one chance I had to be all alone with him and not
worry that I wasn't paying enough attention to my
daughter. We would cuddle, watch *Nick at Nite,* and
have a great time." Still, not all of us are excited about
such 3:00 A.M. love fests. But if you have to be awake,
and if baby allows, catch up on thank-you notes or
arrange photo albums. But don't get involved in anything that might interfere with your getting back to
sleep, such as putting on a pot of high-octane coffee
or getting yourself too deeply immersed in a late night
television program. Once your sleep warden starts to
look drowsy, you're going to want to plunge back into
dreamland as soon as you can. (If your older child
tends to wake up when he hears the baby during the

night, try some "white noise" in his room—a fan, a humidifier or air cleaner, or a tape of calming sounds.)

Don't Forget Dad

Commonly, Dad becomes the primary confidant of the older child in the first couple of weeks after baby's homecoming as Mom and baby fuss with breast-feeding and the quest for sleep. As Michelle illustrates, "I didn't feel as though he wasn't helping or being involved; however, my husband didn't hold our new daughter nearly as much as our first because he was spending time with and entertaining our son."

The situation in Michelle's house is fairly standard for postpartum families of four or more. Dad tends to gravitate toward the older siblings while Mom cares for the newborn. "I definitely have a larger role with the older children than with the baby," Mike, a father of three, explains. "Baby care was more evenly split between us with the first child. Now I tend to focus on the older kids. But even when they are taken care of, I still don't provide adequate focus on the third. I think this is because time is so tight these days. That is, even if the older ones are asleep and the baby isn't complaining, I might tend to work or read an article instead of playing with him."

This arrangement is logistically practical, but may not make for the happiest of families. Dads shouldn't miss out on opportunities to bond with the new baby, and the older child could use some attention from his mom as well. Dividing up this time takes some effort, though. Moms, don't reach automatically for the baby if he's not crying for your breast; let Dad handle some of the postpartum cuddling while you do a puzzle with or read a story to your firstborn.

Asking for Help

There are so many more important things than vacuuming and laundry to be attended to in those first few weeks postpartum—a baby to cuddle, siblings to love and reassure, not to mention the rest and care of your own body. For these reasons, having help around the house with number two is even more crucial than with your first. Where exactly this help is best utilized is an individual thing, but whoever you employ will not likely be bored.

Consider having your own parents, friends, a nanny, or even a doula (see the sidebar on postpartum doulas) to help out the first few days with cleaning, cooking, caring for other children, or watching baby while you catch up with the older child. The nights may seem to last forever, but you'll quickly discover there's never enough time during the day to do all that needs to be done.

Help around the house or a few hours of child care are great gift ideas for a second-time mom. "My girlfriend took my big kids for the afternoon when the baby was about three weeks old," says Alyson. "By then some people may assume you have things under control, but for me, that's when all hell broke loose."

If you prefer to handle the dirty work yourself, set conservative goals. "Focus on the area you spend most of your time, and keep that small area neat," Amy suggests. "Then pick a chore for the day—one thing you know you can do, like sweep only the kitchen, or just scrub the tub, not the whole bathroom. Find what bugs you and keep up on that."

POSTPARTUM DOULAS

More so than with a first child, assistance around the house—whether it's with cooking, cleaning, or lending moral support—is even more crucial when a second baby enters the picture. Since it's not always practical or possible for extended family members to provide this support, many women are discovering that postpartum doulas (not to be confused with labor doulas, who assist women and their partners during childbirth) are a warm and welcome way to simplify those early days at home with a new baby, particularly when there's an older child involved.

Esther's insurance company offered to pay for a doula for twenty hours if she left the hospital after one night rather than two, so since she had a normal delivery and everyone was healthy, she jumped at the chance. "I had the doula come in for four hours a day every other day for the first two weeks," she remembers. "She was wonderful! She cleaned, did laundry, washed dishes, held and changed the baby, played with our three-year-old, and answered the phone. I got my rest and chances to be alone with either the baby or my daughter. I feel like I was able to recover much faster."

Postpartum doulas provide education, support, breast-feeding advice, and nonmedical care to you and your children in your own home. To hook up with a postpartum doula, contact the National Association of Postpartum Care Services (PO Box 1012, Edmonds, WA 98020; 800-45-DOULA).

Nursing Number Two

Of all the delicate situations that arise in those first few postpartum days as a new family, none may confound you quite as much as when you sit down to breast-feed your infant in front of your firstborn. The first time might not be so bad: She will probably be quite interested, ask a lot of questions, and may even want to give it a try. As that first week wears on, though, she may come to resent these interruptions and use intricate tactics to prevent them from recurring, particularly if she doesn't comprehend what's going on.

Preparing your child for the inevitability of these sessions, even weeks before the baby arrives, can help her better accept them later on. Talk about how the baby gets his food from his mommy and that you will need to feed his little brother or sister this way. Tell him that you will need to sit quietly with the baby several times a day. A young firstborn might not clearly understand the implications of this, but it doesn't hurt to give him some fair warning. Eventually the whole scene will become commonplace.

Breast-feeding Battles

When it first becomes evident to your child that this nursing thing is becoming a habit—a habit that takes you away from him eight to ten times a day every day of the week—he may become quite annoyed indeed. In fact, he may come to master the art of "breast-blocking." For instance, you may try to anticipate his needs before you sit down to nurse—say, giving him a snack, putting on his sweater, or setting him up with a video. With a kiss and a smile, you settle down next to him and begin to feed the baby. Before you even feel your milk let down, your child is suddenly too hot, thirsty, and wants to go outside—NOW.

On one occasion, Rebecca remembers asking her three-year-old if he required anything before she started nursing. He asked her to put on his shoes for him, which she did. All seemed calm. "The second the baby latched on, my son ripped his shoes off and began wailing," she says. Not wanting to be replacing shoes every time she breastfed, Rebecca continued to nurse but gently reminded her son that she couldn't help him while the baby was feeding and that he would now have to wait until she was done.

Unless your child is about to swing from your chandelier or otherwise hurt himself, don't completely lose it when he starts acting up when you sit down. You need a tender mix of patience, understanding, and firmness to get through these battles, so stand firm. The baby needs to eat, and your child will have to get used to that. Mealtime tantrums should not be rewarded, but don't lose your temper either—you'll give your child even more reason to detest these frequent distractions. Stay calm and tell him you'll attend to him when you are finished feeding the baby. Tell him that he had the chance to get what he needed before you sat down and that he should think about these things the next time you tell him you are about to nurse.

This might not sink in the first, second, or tenth time you breast-feed in front of your child, but sooner or later the sight will become familiar and he'll realize that the diversion is temporary. Eventually the whole scene will become commonplace. "When my daughter was about three months old I found my twenty-month-old son with his one-piece pajamas unbuttoned and holding an Ernie doll up to his tummy," says Jennifer. "When I asked him what he was doing, he said he was "feeding the baby daddy juice."

Until that happy day, try these tips for heading off feeding-time tantrums:

- Have snacks ready and within your older child's reach.

- Stress all the great things "big kids" can eat that babies can't. Says Esther, "I just told Alyssa that I would be breast-feeding the new baby and that the baby would be getting his milk from mommy's breast. I told her that this is how she used to get food, too. Then we would joke about what babies eat. We would list all the great foods big girls get to eat, like peanut butter and fluff sandwiches, pizza, chicken, and beans, but babies get . . . milk! For breakfast, baby gets . . .

milk! For lunch, baby gets . . . milk! For dinner, baby gets, you guessed it, milk!"

- Get into a routine of reading books or watching a video together *during* nursing times. Ironically, your child may come to think of these as special times together with you rather than times you are out of reach. You may come to appreciate these times as well. "I loved when Madison got hungry," says Aimee. "Trying to rest was the hardest part of those early weeks—there was always something else that needed to be done. But when I had to sit down to nurse, I couldn't do anything else but read to Lyxi and feed Madison. That was the best of times. The three of us would cuddle up together while I read and nursed."

- Make sure the older child gets some special attention when it's not feeding time, some "one-on-one" time of his own.

Tandem Nursing

It is possible to continue nursing an older child when a new baby comes along. Many children lose interest and wean themselves at some point during the pregnancy (see Chapter 4), yet there are those who stick with it right through delivery and after. This can be especially arduous for Mom, who is trying to comfort her firstborn while nourishing her newborn. She may feel guilty about ending the older child's nursing relationship or ambivalent about her own desires. She may also worry that she is interfering with her baby's nutrition in some way.

Ellen found herself nursing her two sons, twenty-five months apart, in the early postpartum days. "My two-year-old nursed all through my pregnancy, although frankly I was hoping that he'd lose interest when the milk supply decreased. This did not happen, nor did the change to colostrum faze him in any way. While I believe in meeting my child's needs—and clearly my two-year-old has a need for the comfort and nurturing he is getting from nursing—I am losing my mind. I cannot nurse the newborn without my older son immediately demanding to nurse. He will not take no for an answer, nor will he be put off, nor will he accept substitute forms of attention. It is very difficult, especially when I need to burp the baby or wipe up spit-up, and my older son will not let go."

Tandem nursing can be physically as well as emotionally draining to a new mother. If the demands seem too much to handle—for instance, if you feel exhausted, extremely irritable, depressed—seriously consider weaning the older child. All the benefits of breast milk aside, neither child will benefit from an increasingly distressed mother.

Women who continue to tandem nurse should keep in mind the following:

- Always let the newborn baby nurse first, particularly in the first week when colostrum is limited in quantity and extremely important to the health of the newborn.

- Eat a variety of nutritious foods and make sure you are getting at least eight glasses of water each day.

- Set limits and stick to them, as Nancy did: "I restricted the two-year-old to the right breast, explaining that the baby would get sick if she didn't get enough milk. I've also told the older child that if we are going to argue about nursing and she can't follow the limits, we will have to stop altogether."

- Consider attending a La Leche League toddler meeting in your area to discuss tandem-nursing issues; call 800-LA-LECHE to find a group in your area.

- Think about cutting back or stopping if tandem nursing seems to exacerbate sibling rivalry in some way. Nursing should be a positive experience for Mom and all of her children.

When it's time to wean your older child, you might try some of these mom-tested tips for easing the transition:

- Give her reasons so that she can understand why she will not be nursing anymore: that it's hard on mother's body or that she's a "big girl" now. She may feel pushed aside if you don't explain why baby can nurse but she can't.

- Agree on a day to stop nursing—let her choose it on a calendar. "We called it a special growing-up day," says Genie. "We got a cake and had another 'birthday' for her. I wrote a poem for her about how it felt to have a growing-up girl."

Emotional Overload

The ups and downs, both physically and emotionally, that accompany a new baby can feel more intense when there's yet another little person to worry about. At a time when a new mom should be feeling proud and blessed, she may be plagued with feelings of depression and guilt.

"I had the baby blues for a week or two after my second child was born," says Joan. "Every time I looked at my son, then age four, I would feel so awful, like I was pushing him away to take care of the baby. I paid a lot of attention to my older son, but I still felt extremely guilty. I would sit at the dining room table and just start crying. My husband would ask what was wrong, and all I could say was that I didn't know. It was too hard to explain. The guilt was overwhelming."

Annie felt the same nagging remorse. "The hardest part about the first six weeks was my baby's constant need to be held, because with an older child in the house, you just can't carry the baby around as much as you did your first. I felt so guilty that I wasn't there for her enough."

Be aware that it's common to feel harried, sad, and

overwhelmed after the birth of a baby—particularly if there are other children adding to your concerns. Persistent crying for no apparent reason, feelings of anger, helplessness, exaggerated highs and lows, substantial changes in your sleep patterns (that you can't blame on the baby), or frightening thoughts (of suicide or hurting the baby) need immediate attention from your doctor. These are signs of postpartum depression, a very common, extremely treatable disorder that affects as many as one in ten mothers.

POSTPARTUM DEPRESSION

Don't suffer alone. The following organizations and resources can help ease the sadness and devastation of postpartum depression.

- Depression After Delivery (PO Box 1282, Morrisville, PA 19067; 800-944-4773 or 215-295-3994): Staffed by volunteers who have experienced some form of postpartum depression, DAD offers support, education, and referrals for women suffering from any symptoms of postpartum depression and for their families.

- Postpartum Adjustment Support Services–Canada (PASS-CAN; Box 7282, Station Main, Oakville, ON L6J 6L6 Canada; fax 905-844-5973): a clearinghouse for support groups, resources, and publications relating to emotional challenges postpartum.

Books

- *After the Baby's Birth . . . A Woman's Way to Wellness: A Complete Guide for Postpartum Women,* by Robin Lim (Celestial Arts, 1991)

- *Mothering the New Mother: Women's Feelings and Needs After Childbirth: A Support and Resource Guide*, by Sally Placksin (Newmarket Press, 1997)

- *The New Mother Syndrome: Coping with Postpartum Stress & Depression*, by Carol Dix (Pocket Books, 1988)

- *Postpartum Survival Guide*, by Ann Dunnewold and Diane G. Sanford (New Harbinger, 1994)

- *Depression After Childbirth: How to Recognize, Treat, and Prevent Postnatal Depression*, by Katharina Dalton and Wendy M. Holton (Oxford University Press, 1996)

- *This Isn't What I Expected: Recognizing and Recovering from Depression and Anxiety After Childbirth*, by Karen R. Kleiman and Valerie D. Raskin (Bantam Doubleday Dell, 1994)

WHEN BABY DOESN'T
COME HOME

They say no two births are exactly alike; however, it was startling to me just how different Sara and Joshua's beginnings played out. Sara's grand entrance was brisk and vital. Josh's was strung along over days (weeks, if you count a bout of preterm labor). Yet it wasn't only their labors and deliveries that contrasted sharply. Sara enjoyed her first few weeks of life eating, growing, and crying lustily each evening. Weak from birth and breathing too quickly, Joshua spent his first five days in our local hospital's neonatal intensive care unit and came home only briefly. On his tenth day of life he was flown to a medical center ninety miles from our home. He arrived there with multiple organ failure and spent the next four weeks in the intensive care nursery.

I had many plans for Sara's first few weeks as a new sibling; however, I hadn't considered that she would be getting acquainted with her little brother during hospital visits or through our nightly discussions about him at the dinner table. I'm sure that his absence was confusing for her. Even when Joshua wasn't the topic of conversation (which was rare)—watching a video, say, or driving in the car, she would ask, "Did Joshua came out of your tummy?"

The baby born too soon or with a critical illness like my son may not come home from the hospital for weeks or even months. For a child who has been anticipating his new sibling's arrival, this can be a distressing time. After months of waiting to become a big brother or sister, all that the child has been looking forward to has been suddenly put on hold.

Assure your child that he or she is still a big brother a sister, but that the baby won't be able to come home until he's well enough. Be sure to explain what's happening in as much detail as your child can handle. If possible, bring him to the hospital to visit his new baby. The tubes and wires may seem scary to you, but if you don't use that word when describing what they are going to see, young children who don't understand their implications may simply find them interesting.

With a sibling in the hospital, there are bound to be a lot of sad feelings and frustration at home. Here are some tips for making it easier for the whole family:

- Don't put on a constant happy face around your child if you're not feeling that way. Let your child see that it is okay to be sad, worried, or angry about the situation. However, for your child's sake, try to talk about any positive developments and find some hope with every day.

- Don't underestimate your child's ability to understand

the situation. Be honest and answer his questions directly.

- Have your child draw pictures or pick out photographs to place in the baby's isolette at the hospital.

- Try to spend some "normal" time with your child—go to the zoo, have dinner out, take him to a movie, have a picnic in the park. Your spirits, too, could use the lift.

- Explain that the baby's problems are not in any way his fault. Some children develop guilt feelings in these situations and need to be reassured.

- If you are too despondent to properly care for your child, be sure to arrange for some help for both of you. Have a sitter or relative spend some quality time with him. If you find you are unable to care for your other child without crying or are unable to handle routine tasks, ask your doctor about finding professional help.

- If your baby's condition turns grave, it can be difficult to know just what to tell your other child, particularly in your own state of grief. Enlist family and friends to field phone calls and stay available to comfort your child. Don't turn away from each other in these trying times. Answer your child's questions honestly and assure him of your undying love for him.

These early days as a new family may seem long and tiring, but that's probably more a reflection of too little sleep and the equivalent of a hormonal curveball than a taste of what the future will entail. The issues at hand—breast-feeding, sleeping, spending time with your older child—may seem pivotal at this moment, when in fact these simple acts will become routine as the days pass. In a short time things will begin to click again.

Right now you all need to simmer a bit. You've been thrown together quite abruptly and there's bound to be some tension. Take it slow, and don't let the heat get to you. You can handle it. You're a family now.

9

Stepping Up to Siblinghood

> *"Cody's first smiles were for Ben, not for me," Jeanette explains. "I don't remember when that started happening—I think it was about the time Cody was a month or so old. He would be in his bouncer or on the floor and Ben would get down level with him and start talking. Cody would smile and coo at him. They had wonderful conversations. They really seemed to understand each other."*

You can attempt to guess how your son or daughter will react to the new arrival. After all, you've known your child all of his or her young life and you probably have a pretty good idea how he or she reacts to challenges. However, this is one of the most heavily loaded situations you'll ever observe. New beds, new houses, other life changes, are hard but bearable because his or her parents' love stays constant. But baby compromises the one given children could count on.

Before the new baby was born, you might have wondered, "How will I ever find enough love for two kids?" The answer is probably obvious to you now, but your firstborn is pondering that same question with a little more uncertainty. Whether or not it's the truth, it's likely that your child will think that there's just not as much love to go around these days. Your job is to assure him that, in fact, there's more than there was before the baby came.

The road to siblinghood is rocky and littered with rest stops that don't have bathrooms. That is to say, it's challenging, frustrating, and can wreak havoc with previously mastered toileting habits. Toddlers in particular, who thrive on routine, will get more than jostled if a new baby completely disrupts The Way Things Work. Strap yourself in for a wild ride.

Coping Mechanisms

Think about how hard it has been for you to adjust your life and your expectations to this new, expanded family. Well, here's your child, busily trying to figure out who she is and what's going on around her, and you throw her this fussy, needy curveball. There are several ways a newly promoted sibling might field this pitch, and you should expect to encounter all of them at some point in the first few months.

Regression

Don't be surprised if your long-weaned two-year-old wants to breast-feed, your three-year-old wants to drink from a bottle, your four-year-old starts wetting her pants, or your six-year-old won't go to sleep at his usual bedtime. Before he realizes how good he has it, your child may think that being a baby is pretty cool: getting picked up whenever you cry, having Mom and Dad's attention any hour of the day, the toys and stuffed animals that seem to arrive in a steady stream. By becoming a "baby" again, your child can enjoy the attention and comfort these behaviors bring—or so he thinks.

All of these behaviors are your child's way of re-
minding you that he or she still needs your care and attention. So don't brush them off, and don't scold or criticize
him for being human. In fact, if you go ahead and give
in to some of these requests, you might find them very
short-lived. "When Shawn was born, my almost-four-
year-old wanted to nurse," says Lisa. "I think it was a
couple of days after the birth, so I let him. He tasted the
colostrum and said, 'Yuk! I want milk from the fridge,
okay, Mom?' He never asked again."

Once Renée started giving baby Isaac bottles, Hannah
(age three) was eager to try them again too, even though
she hadn't touched one since her first birthday. "I gave
her some formula and that was the end of that," she remembers. "She spit it all over the room and wiped her
tongue vigorously with a towel."

Pay heed to these signals for a bit more affection, but
firmly remind him of all the perks of being a "big kid."
In time he will realize that diapers and formula are not
as enticing as they seem, and that riding bikes, painting,
swimming, and swinging beat a burp and a bath any day.
(If your child is under six, read *I Wish I Was the Baby*, by
DJ Long.) So let him take a sip of the baby's bottle or
chomp on a pacifier (disinfect well afterward) if he's insistent. Says Alyson, whose firstborn liked to climb up into
her lap and have her feed her from a cup, "I think they
have to work out their problems, too, in their own way.
They need to feel that they can have these feelings and
you will accept them no matter what."

Obsession

The first time we visited our friends' new baby, their
almost-two-year-old daughter—a frequent playmate of
our daughter's—had a raging fit if Sara so much looked
at one of her toys. It was as if the new baby had come
along and taken everything that was previously hers, and

she now saw a desperate need to hang on to whatever she could.

Children might also express fears or nightmares, or have trouble sleeping. Again, take your child's disturbances seriously, but don't go overboard. If a child who previously slept through the night begins getting extra attention and care for waking up in the wee hours, a very unrestful pattern may develop. Try to get your child to talk about bothersome fears or, if he is truly not old enough to put these into words, encourage role-playing or use puppets to have him explain what's bothering him. Frequent nightmares or night terrors (fearful screaming, flailing episodes that are often accompanied by sleepwalking) may require a doctor's attention.

Aggression

Ashleigh was taken aback by her son's assaults on the new baby. "Lucas was fifteen months old when Kimmy was born. When she first came home, he got a lot whinier and a little distant—quieter sometimes, tantrums others. More tense, I guess. He's always been pretty easygoing, but he was hitting the baby a lot. I tried explaining to him that it hurt to hit her, but he either didn't understand or didn't care. I got a lot more tense too, trying not to get upset with him and keep things under control. I had expected negativity, but not so much aggression."

While it may be easier to imagine a young boy hitting a sibling out of frustration, such a physical reaction isn't reserved for males. "There was a lot of squeezing, pinching, and roughhousing when Ari came along," Sue B. says about Ilana, who was two and a half at the time. "She would say, 'I love you, Ari,' and at the same time be twisting his leg. In hindsight I think I may have made the situation worse. My emotional/hormonal instincts took over and I wanted to protect the baby, so I would constantly be pulling her off him. Now I think I was not giving her a chance to form a relationship with him."

Sue's instincts to protect the baby were right on target. Under no circumstances should the older child be allowed to hit, slap, or even threaten the baby. The trick for parents is not to overreact or to become aggressive in response to the behavior. According to Dr. Benjamin Spock, shaming or punishing the child can backfire. An aggressive child may then worry that his parents no longer love him because of his feelings, then bottle up the jealousy. This in turn may exaggerate his aggressive impulses. Instead, "tackle" him with love and understanding. Acknowledge and accept his feelings, but state the rules clearly.

Depression

Instead of acting out toward the new baby, a child may turn his anger inward. He may seem sad or tired, or lose his appetite. Suddenly he won't have anything to do with his favorite toys or play outside when he has the chance. He may plop down in front of videos for hours on end.

It may be easier to overlook an emotionally hurting child who is not in your face or taunting the baby. In fact, his quietude can seem pretty darn convenient. It may take an extra effort on your part, but be sure to give your child your focused time and attention daily. He may need encouragement to become involved with the baby's care, but once he sees that you need him after all, he may be more eager to help.

If you notice that sleeping or eating habits are severely affected, or if he avoids activities that he previously enjoyed for several days, it's a good idea to put in a call to your pediatrician.

The Many Faces of a New Sibling

Your firstborn may surprise you with his reaction to the new baby. He may become the newborn's biggest advocate, hugging and kissing with fervor, "protecting" him from visitors or strangers at the mall. On the other hand, he may refuse to acknowledge the baby's presence, or become quietly withdrawn. You may see sides of her—angry, violent, sweetly touching—that you've never before witnessed. And these are all on the *first* day.

Take a look at some real-life sibling reactions and some strategies for working through them.

Just Try to Love Me

In the first week or two, your older child may test your devotion by being difficult, stubborn, and generally unpleasant to be around. Recalls Esther, "For a few days Alyssa reverted to wanting to fight and argue about everything, from which color plate and cup to use to which pajamas she was going to wear."

Frustrating as this may be, a child needs to assert whatever minute vestiges of control he can. For a few days, at least, let him take the wheel if the requests aren't unreasonable. Arguing over colors of plastic ware is a waste of everyone's energies. And the more he learns to do for himself, the better—independence is a valuable trait for big siblings. By staying calm yourself, you may help divert a major meltdown.

Temper, Temper

Amy's daughter Alice lapsed into full-blown tantrums when new sister Caroline came home. "I really had to be tough with her; even though I wanted to hug and cuddle her and be sympathetic, that just made it all much worse.

It was as if her brain were exploding, and all I could do was stand back."

As Amy discovered, sometimes a new sibling needs to blow off some jealous, frustrated steam, and there's nothing you can do to stop it. So let her erupt—but don't encourage it. "I acted like I'd always acted, unsympathetic towards her tantrums. I'd lug her upstairs and have her stay there until she calmed down." Between tantrums, Amy tried to read to Alice and spend as much extra time with her as she could.

Tough Love

"Before the baby came along, I was worried about the rivalry aspects. But now my problem is just the opposite. My three-year-old is so excited that the new baby is here that she constantly wants to hold, feed, change, touch her," says Andrea. "This wouldn't be bad except that the baby has colic all day long, so we are always trying to calm her and get her to sleep. As soon as we accomplish one of these things, the three-year-old wakes her up with a loving embrace, and another round of crying begins. We don't want to discourage her from loving her sister, but we are constantly telling her no or losing our temper with her when she wakes the baby up."

Renée experienced a similar reaction from her three-year-old when Isaac first came home. "Hannah was constantly in his face in the early days after his birth. It seemed as if she wanted to breathe his air." Not wanting Hannah to resent the baby simply because they were being overprotective, they set forth a rule: If he doesn't look unhappy or isn't crying, she could do as she pleased in terms of hovering. In Andrea's case, she might have added "sleeping" to the hands-off rule. "In retrospect, I think Isaac rather liked the attention," Renée adds.

The Green-Eyed Sibling

"My oldest, eighteen months when her sister was born, definitely had a case of jealousy for a while," Kayleen explains. "Every time I sat down to nurse the baby, she would want to crawl into my lap as well, or would sit down on the ground and burst into tears! She didn't want me to spend time alone with the baby. One time we were trying to take pictures of the two girls, and she kept pushing the baby off her lap! Fortunately we were there to catch her!"

It can be hard to see your child hurting and envious, but it's a completely natural and expected reaction to the arrival of a new sibling. That said, parents shouldn't try to discourage these emotions simply because they aren't "happy" or "positive." Children need to learn that whatever they feel about the new baby—sad, frustrated, jealous, angry—you'll love them just the same. More even.

There's not too much you can do to help your child besides earn her trust back gradually. Acknowledge her feelings verbally and with tender hugs. Remind her of your love every day and surprise her with affection every now and then—she'll come around. "She gradually got better and better, and is now fine most of the time," Kayleen continues. "Sometimes she wants a hug in between switching sides nursing, but then she lets me get back to it."

Playing Nice

Someone once told me that the most dangerous thing in a newborn's home is a toddler. I'm not talking premeditated aggression here. On the contrary, the most awestruck, adoring sibling can harm a baby with his affection. Full of energy, enthusiasm, and interest, young children often don't understand the tender fragility of a baby. Perhaps you gave your two-year-old a baby doll in the weeks before her sibling was born, to feed and diaper and cuddle for "practice." If so, you probably also observed your child dragging the thing around by its hair or found the doll naked at the bottom of her toy chest or on the floor of your car.

Chances are your child wasn't being malicious with dolly; she was just being a toddler. And that's the scary part. A toddler who just wants to share a toy with his brother may fling it at him with glee. Another who thinks baby will have more fun playing on his tummy than his back may roll him with excessive abandon. A generous three-year-old might feel proud to want to share his building blocks with his newly grasping baby sister—his hard, sharp-edged, heavy building blocks.

All good reasons for never leaving them alone together. But here on Earth, there will be times you may need to step out of the room for a nanosecond or twelve. Children need to know how to be gentle with a baby at all times, especially during those brief instances when you turn your head. If your child is old enough to try to pull your bottom lip over the top of your head (about eight months or so), you start teaching him, "No, *gentle*. Be nice."

Once a child can understand those words, dolls are excellent for preparational purposes as well—show kids how to handle them gently, softly. And then when baby's home, you can demonstrate, frequently, the right ways to touch or hold him. Children are infinitely curious about their new sibling, so give them the chance to get to know the baby while you observe: Involve your child in diapering, bathing, and dressing his new sibling, making it clear it's okay to touch the baby if you do so carefully.

Still, you should do some toddler-proofing, just to be sure. When baby's asleep, keep crib rails up and stools or other climbables out of baby's room. Keep tabs on your toddler while baby's napping so you don't get any surprises. And start teaching your toddler early on that his toys are his only. Sharing is great when you're supervising, but "Ages Three and Up" applies to all the children in the room, not just the one playing at the moment.

Age or Rage?

The terrible twos can be draining enough without throwing a baby into the ring. "The behavioral changes with my son were very gradual," says Michelle, "so much so that I don't even know if I can attribute them to having a sister or if it was just his age." Between ages two to four, when children are prone to tantrums and still have trouble verbalizing what's bothering them, it can be hard to tell if it's jealousy, anger, frustration, hurt feelings, or a natural by-product of growing up that's sending him into a tailspin.

Most likely it's a combination of all of those. Even if the baby hadn't appeared, your child might have been as whiny, fussy, and uncooperative as he is now, for some other reason (for instance, you put his juice in the blue cup instead of the red one). Shaking up the house with a new sister certainly won't make things any better. Try to deal with the developmental fallout as best you can, whatever the underlying reasons. Give him words to put to his feelings. Let his tantrums run their course, but don't condone them. Do whatever you might do if a baby weren't babbling in the background. Lots of hugs may help, too.

The Curiosity Factor

Babies are extraordinarily interesting to children. They love to feel their heads, touch their noses, and pull at their legs. That's why, no matter how well behaved your older child may be, he shouldn't be left alone with the baby in the early months, particularly if the older child is under age four. Even the kindest, gentlest toddlers can hug, pat, or cuddle the baby with just a wee too much zeal. Not to mention the curiosity factor, that driving force that compels small people toward dirty and dangerous situations. Left alone with a baby, a well-meaning toddler may wonder, "Can I fit my teddy bear in his mouth?" "What kind of noise will he make if I bite him?" or "Do his toes come off?"

The Happy Surprise

New siblings aren't screaming, hitting, and digging out pacifiers all over the country. Every now and then there will be a child who surprises his parents with his positive grasp of the situation. "I had heard a lot of horror stories about older siblings' reactions," says Joan. "But overall, my son was much better than I thought he would be."

There's bound to be some emotional fallout to suddenly having to share your parents with another small person. But not all children act out because of the changes. And certainly a good percentage aren't as devastated as their parents had expected they would be. Families that put a lot of effort into preparing their child to be a sibling and are clear about what they should expect might see fewer problems later on, but nothing's guaranteed. The older the child, too, the easier it may be for her, since she's bound to have interests of her own and require less focused attention from her parents.

BIG-KID BENEFITS

Becoming a big sibling is a proud and exciting honor. However, your firstborn may be too caught up in what he can't have or what he thinks he's losing to appreciate all that he stands to gain. You can help your child step into his new role by acknowledging his concerns while continuing to stress all the great things about being a big brother or sister. Some tactics:

- Give your child a new privilege as a brother or sister, such as staying up later or earning an extra book at bedtime.

- Help him feel more capable by putting his juice boxes on a low shelf and putting his cups and flatware in a

reachable drawer so he can get them himself. Show
him how to brush his teeth—and praise him when he
does these things completely on his own.

- Make sure one parent (or both, if you can swing it)
takes him on a big-kid outing once every week or so,
no babies allowed. Got to a movie, to Discovery Zone,
to a children's museum—places where a baby in tow
might otherwise slow you down.

- The older child may try to side with you rather than
the baby at this age, taking on "policing" (tattletale)
or teacher roles with his little sib. This is a fine way
for children to feel older and important. But be sure to
allow him to become a kid again whenever teddy calls.

As "big" as your first might seem compared to the
baby, be sure to keep his age in perspective. "I lost patience with some of my son's behaviors," says Mary.
"Stuff that I accepted and had time for before we had our
second suddenly felt intolerable. Because the baby was so
tiny and helpless and demanding, and my almost-three-
year-old so big and capable by contrast, I suddenly really,
really wanted the older one to be able to do more things
for himself. My expectations for him went through the
roof without my noticing it. At the same time he began
to act more babylike. The way I was treating him, I think
he got the idea that being a big boy was a crummy deal
after all. I had to carefully assess whether my expectations
of the older one were realistic—and accept that he was
still just a little one himself."

Help Him Help You

Conveniently, one of the most successful ways to help
children through the household changes associated with

a new sibling is to get them involved in the baby's care. Fortunately, your child will most likely enjoy helping out with new-baby chores just as much as you will appreciate having him do so. Giving him the chance to participate in diaper changes, feedings, and general soothing procedures will boost his self-esteem and let him feel that you still need him around.

Beware of setting up the child too much, however. "It's important not to overemphasize all the help a sibling can provide, because in the beginning, it's not realistic," Sue B. says. Her daughter, Ilana, was almost six when her second brother, Noah, was born. "Everyone was telling her what a big help she was going to be when the baby was born, but once he got here, there wasn't all that much she could do with him initially—especially since I'm breast-feeding. I think this was related to her poking and prodding him a lot—trying to figure out what her relationship to him was. Once Noah turned one month and could focus a little bit, she could talk to him and stop him from crying, and that began to help."

Your older child doesn't need to be very big to feel like a big brother or sister. Even a two-year-old will feel "grown up" compared to a sibling who can't run after a ball, color with a crayon, or eat a waffle by himself.

Here are baby-friendly ways your older children can help out:

- Diaper changes: Set up a diaper-changing station at a low level, perhaps on a quilt in the family room or baby's bedroom, so that your child can assist you more easily. She can fetch diapers, unbutton baby's clothing (with your approval), apply diaper-rash ointments, discard used diapers or deal with cloth ones appropriately. If she can master the technique and is willing, let her change diapers on her own.

- Feedings: Older children can fetch water or pillows for Mom when it's time for breast-feeding, or supplies for bottle-feeding. (Better not to encourage them to try giving the baby a bottle on their own just yet.) They might also come to recognize this as a time to sit quietly with Mom or hold a book for her to read aloud.

- Soothing: If you take the time to explain to your children why babies cry, they may be more tolerant and even helpful when he begins to wail. Many children enjoy running down "the list" of what could be bothering the newborn and will try to help soothe him. If you allow a child to hold the baby, prop a pillow under the baby's head. This gives the infant some extra support and takes some of the weight off the child's arms.

- Playtime: As baby reaches milestones in the first few months, let your older child have fun with her new developments. For instance, she can try to make the baby smile by smiling first, have the baby follow a toy with her eyes, teach her to bring her hands together, play peekaboo.

By all means, don't pressure a child to get involved if he really doesn't want to. Nagging him to help with the baby might only make him more resentful of the infant's arrival. Your child will tell you how much he wants to get involved. Be a good listener.

BOOKS ABOUT SIBLINGS

These books about siblings deal with life with a sibling, rather than getting accustomed to a new baby in the house.

- *Big Help!*, by Anna Grossnickle Hines (Clarion Books, 1995). Sam can't seem to do anything without little sister Lucy wailing, "Me help." More often than not, Lucy's help is just the opposite. Rather than getting upset with his little sister, though, Sam finds a way for her to help him that makes him feel proud and lets him finish coloring his picture.

- *My Little Brother*, by Debi Gliori (Candlewick Press, 1992). A little girl is so fed up with her pesky little brother that she wishes he would disappear. Vanishing cream, feeding him to a "wild beast," and sending him to the moon don't help. One night when he's missing from his crib, she worries that he has indeed disappeared and remembers how nice and how small he really is. When she finds him asleep in the closet, she never wants him to leave again.

- *We're Very Good Friends, My Brother and I*, by P. K. Hallinan (Ideals Children's Books, 1990). Two brothers enjoy each others' companionship, going for long walks, running fast, pretending to fly, and acting creepy. And even though they don't always see eye to eye about everything, "being together beats being alone." A delight for very young children and early readers.

Managing Two (or More)

"The hardest part of the day-to-day routine is managing to go anywhere," says Michelle. "Just as everyone is fed, showered, and dressed, it's time for the baby's nap. She gets up and it's time for lunch, getting cleaned up, and by then the toddler is rubbing his eyes. Plus the concept of packing the diaper bag, lugging the car seat—it's no wonder I never seem to get my errands done."

You are already aware that one child puts a "crimp" in the lifestyle you once enjoyed. Well, two kids will tie it in knots. Even your most basic daily activities become a major challenge, at least at first. If both of your kids are very young, just going to the supermarket, for instance, can involve skilled maneuvering of strollers and slings, a keen eye, and a cartful of patience.

If the older sibling is out of diapers, or in elementary school, things may be easier in some ways, but getting around is still no piece of cake. You can sometimes count on his help during retail outings or at doctor's visits. Left alone with the two of them on a rainy afternoon, however, it can be difficult to find an activity that will keep both of them amused.

But guess what. You will get through these days. Eventually you'll get your shopping done, and you might even manage to eat something. It's certainly not going to be fun *all* of the time, but what a rush when things work out!

Why Did One Seem So Hard?

Spend your first day with two kids and you'll no doubt wonder, "This is out of hand. Why did I think one child was so hard to manage?"

The reason is that one child *was* exhausting. You were inexperienced. You had no idea that an actual person could survive on three hours of sleep at a stretch. And you thought projectile vomiting was merely an exaggeration.

But even after you adjusted to the constant flow of bodily fluids, you were probably still reeling from the lifestyle changes a new baby inflicts. Your first child redefines your whole life, gathering everything you once found important into a pile and reshuffling the deck. Your first child redefines *you*.

Relationships can also take a beating during this time. With the first baby, you are both adjusting to new parent roles and figuring out who is responsible for what and when, and "whose idea it was to have kids anyway," as Renée puts it. "Ed and I were both really vile at times over the subject of getting some alone time," she says. "By the time the second baby came along, all those creases were pretty much ironed out."

So while two (or more) kids may be physically more exhausting and a bit harder to juggle, it's less of a transformation. With a second child you are not so much reshaping yourself and your relationship as you are "polishing" them.

Why Two Isn't as Hard as You Think

Friends (or those who think they are) may tell you that second children are more than twice as much work. In some ways that may be true. There are a lot of chores, a lot of maintenance required, when you've got two offspring. But in a lot of ways the transition is easier than you might expect.

For one thing, the learning curve is shorter. This time you have the experience to know what lies ahead and the hindsight to know it won't last long. You'll find that you fall back into the new-baby routine more quickly than you imagined. Who knows? You might even handle the middle-of-the-night feedings with more aplomb as well.

Moreover, you've got an extra helper this round. True, this helper might seem more of a hindrance at times, but when you're holding a poopy baby up by his ankles and you realize the diapers are across the room, you may feel differently.

This time you have different priorities. One child seemed hard because it was uncharted territory. You tried hard to attain perfection and chided yourself when you (inevitably) could not. As a second-timer, you know that there is no such thing as perfection. With two children, there will be mistakes, there will be tears, a few spills, and some very stinky smells. This time you are based in reality. Your goal is to love your children as best you can—and *perhaps* make it to the market. Here's how.

Mastering the Turmoil

You've got the experience. You've got bibs and wipes. You can handle anything, right? Well, there's a lot going on in your new, improved household. You've got a newborn (enough said), his or her somewhat bewildered sibling, their recovering, sleep-deprived mother, an equally exhausted father, and relatives you haven't seen in years calling to see how the baby is. With so many factors in play, your household may seem to spin out of control. But it doesn't have to.

Follow these suggestions for taking charge of the day-to-day mini dramas and actually get something done:

- Set goals. Make that mini goals. Not "lose twenty pounds" or "redecorate living room." I'm talking "give baby a bath," "do a load of laundry," or "buy groceries."

- Become a list maker. One for your daily goals (see the preceding suggestion), one for reminders, one for useful telephone numbers, and so on. With no more than three consecutive hours of sleep, capricious hormone levels, and diapers up to *here*, do you think you'll remember when those library books are due?

- Divide and conquer. If at any point there are two adults in the house, each can grab one for some solid one-on-one time. Most likely there will be some chorelike duties involved, such as diaper changing, food preparation, baths, toy cleanup. What does it matter? Your child will love the attention, even if you're just taking out the trash together.

- Have a stash of special books or toys at the ready for when you need to focus on the baby and your other child isn't cooperating. But be careful not to "train" your child to act out by offering goodies as rewards at these times. This is meant to create an easy diversion for you that your child will enjoy.

- Plan on your child watching more television. Oh, don't make a face. It's not forever, and it doesn't have to be *Power Rangers*. *Sesame Street* is on several times during the day. (Choose *one*.) Even better, stock up on videos that agree with both of you. You may find yourself on the couch alongside your firstborn, breast-feeding or cuddling the baby. (By the way, if you haven't seen

it, give Disney's *Toy Story* a try. It may not have babies
in it, but it's basically about a child's favorite toy—
Woody—who suddenly feels threatened and displaced
when a brand-new shiny toy—Buzz Lightyear—moves
in. Remind you of anything? Of course, in the end,
there's plenty of room, and adoration, for both of
them.)

- Help older kids learn to entertain themselves. One of
  Kayleen's keys to survival, she says, is "room time.
  My toddler plays in her room by herself at least a half
  hour to an hour every day. That gives me time to
  spend with the baby alone or do housework, have
  breakfast, make phone calls, read the paper. She loves
  playing in her room and doing her own thing. I'm
  already working with the baby on amusing herself in
  the bouncy chair, on a blanket, or in a playpen on
  her own."

- Become a matchmaker. Look at it from your older
  child's point of view—how much fun can a newborn
  (yawn) and her worn-out mom be, anyway? If possible, try to set up periodic play dates for your older
  child. She gets to play with a peer, and you get to talk
  to a real live grown-up.

- Look for the humor. There are a lot of trying situations
  that make us think, "Someday we'll look back on this
  and laugh." Well, why wait? Sometimes a good guf-
  faw can relieve the tension of an otherwise overwhelming situation. You don't want to encourage
  dangerous or defiant (or what seems like disloyal) behavior with an approving smile, but sometimes things
  get so ridiculous that you can choose either laughing
  or exploding. Choose the former.

- Get organized. If you haven't mastered this skill yet,
  this is the time to get up to speed. Invest in containers
  of all shapes and sizes, and find a place for everything.
  Have one for art supplies, one for play foods, one for
  sippy cups, a basket for baby's toys, and so on. Kids

can become more self-reliant when things have defined storage areas and may even enjoy returning things to their proper places.

- Certain chores are inevitable, but don't let them get in the way of enjoying your kids. The dust bunnies can grow a little plumper when a sunny afternoon beckons a picnic. The bunnies will wait for you. Breezy afternoons won't.

Outings

Never before has a supermarket represented such terror to an individual, nor a meal at a restaurant seemed quite so elusive. Many of the activities you take for granted with one child—grocery shopping, eating out, getting a haircut, going to the doctor—become challenging tests of courage and character with two. Even if you can manage logistically—what with strollers, backpacks, diaper bags, and string cheese—how do you keep both children quietly amused throughout the affair? And should things begin to blow, how can you keep your cool in front of dozens of strangers?

Still, you see people out there, shopping, eating, getting on with their lives, children in tow. What do they know that you don't? For one thing, if you see a family with one adult for every child, take them out of the running. That's as good as cheating. What we're discussing here are the brave souls who must tote or push a newborn, praying that he doesn't wake up/get hungry/poop/ develop colic, all while trying to keep up with a preschooler hell-bent on darting around and through the clothing racks or filling up your shopping cart with every purple product in the store.

These parents know this might happen, but they are out there anyway. That's because such a scene is rare. Or at least, it doesn't have to be the norm. The hardest outing will likely be your first. That attempt is usually prompted by a mini emergency, such as a serious milk shortage or a sudden doctor's appointment. For my family, the first time we went out to dinner as a family was not by choice. A devastating snowstorm that knocked out our electricity for four days sent us packing to a far-off hotel with Sara, then two and a half, and our six-weeker, Josh. For some reason, we even attempted dinner out at a fairly nice restaurant (no crayons or play spaces). The baby slept the entire time and Sara was enthralled by the restaurant's breadsticks. (She also had a fever, which subdued her somewhat.) My point is, we didn't have much of a choice, so we gave it a try, and it went just fine.

Chances are your first experiences won't be half as bad as you expect. Then you'll try again, and learn from your errors, and eventually you and your kids will be sailing through the mall with the best of them.

Food Forays

It didn't used to be such a production. You walked around the corner or got in your car and popped over to the grocery store. Maybe you had to first remember where you left the coupons. Add one child to the equation and the outing becomes a bit more complicated, but doable. You learn not to schedule this excursion just before naptime (unless she would sleep through the trip) or when she is particularly hungry. Not too difficult.

Now you've got two of them. Unless there are two of *you*, you're outnumbered. First hurdle: the logistics. Who goes where? According to the Universal Shopping Cart Law, if your child is not forced to sit in the specially designed cart seat, he will ultimately ask either to ride in the cart basket, leaving little room for food (the reason you're there in the first place), or to hang off the front of the cart. If you give in to this latter request (usually just before you break down and let him have a cookie from the bakery just before dinnertime), the child will, of course, try to get off the cart when you're not looking, resulting in an "owie" as well as embarrassing stares from other supermarket patrons.

The trick to managing the market with two kids is to start out small and gain confidence. Don't make a big deal of it. Strap them in the double stroller and run in for some milk on the way home. Have your money in an easy-to-reach pocket and get it done with. Next time work up to fruit, then maybe some frozen foods. (Note: Do not attempt the deli counter on a Saturday afternoon until you are certified.)

As for supermarket seating, you have several options, but you need to experiment a bit to find the best fit, as Jeanette discovered. "First I put Ben, nineteen months, in the cart seat and three-month-old Cody's carrier in the basket. But where do the groceries go? Then I put Cody in the sling, but Ben keeps poking him while I push the cart. Cody gets mad because all he can see is Ben. Or else Ben is handing everything in the cart to Cody, which makes the sling get really heavy! Then I put Ben in the sling and use the cart with the baby seat on it. Well, Ben gets tired of the sling in the store, as he can't reach anything, so he winds up fussing. So we dance to the Muzak and people think I'm nuts. Oh well. We tried Cody in the baby seat and Ben walking—ONCE. I think I'll need track shoes to attempt that again! This time Ben helped to push and didn't slow down the whole way through the store. Every time I tried to stop to get something off the shelf, he was loading everything he could reach into the basket."

An increasing number of thoughtful supermarkets, as well as toy and discount stores, own a limited fleet of carts with a baby seat attached crosswise over the basket, which leaves the usual seat available for your other child. These might work for you.

Some parents of toddlers and preschoolers favor "leashes" to keep them in line. They aren't for everyone, but surely they can help if you have a very busy, curious child and you need to focus your attention on something for a minute or two. Better perhaps to teach "heeling" (to continue the dog metaphor for a moment). Children need to learn not to run wildly through public places, so the sooner you instill this thought, the better. In fact, if you're organized enough to begin practicing this *before* the baby's born, you'll be ahead of the game once you attempt a shopping trip en masse.

Eating Out

One of the riskiest destinations for a family of four or more is the "nice" restaurant. Remember? You started avoiding *these* places shortly after that episode when you spent an hour toting your firstborn around the parking lot. Your partner, meanwhile, sheepishly finished his or her salad and asked for the rest of the meal "to go."

With two kids, the "steaks" are higher. Now there are four of you who have to get through dinner without crying. Nonetheless, it is still possible to have a pleasant evening out. As always, this is highly dependent upon everyone's moods. If you're in the early days, when many babies are rocked to sleep by car engines, you may be able to get through an entire dinner before he wakes from the trip. But as he gets older and requires holding/feeding/entertainment, you will need more skillful tactics.

If you previously enjoyed dining out, do make the effort on occasion. You shouldn't assume you have to spend both children's toddler years in Chuck E. Cheese because of one bad restaurant experience. There are plenty of restaurants bridging the gap between Burger King and Lutece, where both hot dogs and filet mignon are served with pride. Check your local paper or the parents' guide to your area for family-friendly restaurant reviews. Then follow these tips for dining without tears:

- Call ahead if you are concerned about bringing kids to a particular restaurant. It's also a good idea to make a reservation or get on a waiting list before you leave your house, especially on a weekend evening.

- Eat at "fringe" times—late lunches, early dinners—when the restaurants are less crowded and waitpeople are less harried.

- Bring a couple of snack items if you have particularly fussy eaters. You don't want to be ordering dish after dish trying to please your kids.

- Don't forget crayons and little notepads or stickers to keep kids busy while they wait for food.

- If restaurant outings prove more frustrating than enjoyable, order in some pizza, wait a month or two to try again, and in the meantime spend your dining-out budget on the two of you.

Dining In

As nice as it is to have someone else do the cooking and cleaning up, most of your meals will be eaten at home. For busy parents of two or more, creating healthy, palatable meals—and getting the kids to eat them—is no piece of cake. Planning and preparation are the keys to making mealtimes work.

- Create menus. Once a week, make a list of breakfasts, lunches, and dinners for the next seven days. (Don't forget kids' meals.) Write out a shopping list and stick to it. The idea here is to minimize those emergency trips to the market on the way home from work. Those "quick trips" are not so quick when everyone in your town has also run out of milk.

- Simplify meals. Prepare foods, or parts of recipes, in advance so that you are not starting from scratch when you walk in the door: freeze casseroles, soups, cut-up vegetables.

- Buy in bulk (but only if you can eat all of the food before it goes bad!). Or buy several packages of something you use often (juice boxes, pastas, rice, soups, salad dressings).

- Cook larger portions of dishes that can be frozen or packed in lunches the next day. (Don't reheat food more than once, though.)

- Have breakfast foods in an easy-to-reach location; encourage children to fetch their own (unless doing so would make you all late for work and school).

- Trade off meal preparation with your partner on designated days.

- Decide how many take-out meals you can afford, and work them into your weekly plans. Think pizza.

- Invest in a few easy-to-follow cookbooks for some fresh ideas.

- When dinnertime arrives, feed the baby first so that you can attempt a normal meal with the rest of the family. When the baby is about eight or nine months old, he can sit in a high chair with the rest of you and sample your dinners—let him try soft breads, soft, shredded chicken, very small pieces of cheese, mashed potatoes, tofu.

Other Outings

Doctor's appointments, clothes-shopping trips, zoo excursions, play groups—they will all become manageable with time and practice. A few pointers for easier outings:

- Take note of your children's "best times," and schedule outings and play dates for these hours. Mornings usually find children more agreeable than late afternoons, which tend to accumulate the effects of hunger and fatigue.

- Arm yourself with snacks, portable toys, other temporary diversions.

- Restock your outing bag every night with diapers, wipes, lotion, changes of clothing, sunscreen, for more efficient mobilization each day.

- Take extra care in parking lots or crossing busy streets, especially when your hands are full of baby seats and packages. Older kids may try to make a break for it!

- Stay flexible. When running errands, tend to necessities first in case your trip gets cut short. It will happen.

Must-Have Gear

There is definitely less to buy when your second child arrives. You are probably set with cribs, stretchies, swings, and other hand-me-down baby equipment. So what's missing this time?

On the Go

If you have a child under three, consider a double stroller even if your firstborn hasn't ridden in one since he could walk. There's a big jealousy factor at play here, which you'll realize the first time you buckle your newborn into his own stroller. What's more, you can't chase a toddler through the clothing racks at the mall—and they know that. There are leashes and there are strollers. Take your pick. Your child may not want to ride in it constantly, but that leaves more room for packages, diaper bags, blankets, and backpacks.

An ongoing debate amongst double-stroller pushers is side-by-side seating versus the front-back version. The side-by-side models let the kids amuse each other—great if they are close in age. Both kids have an unobstructed view and can recline in their seats comfortably. The downside of these models is that they can be harder to steer through doorways. The front-back versions, on the other hand, are slimmer and somewhat more maneuverable, but the seating can start fights ("No, I want to sit in front!") and can leave one child more prone to having his hair pulled.

Siblings over three might be more suited to the variety of "sit and stroll" models available, such as the Sit 'N' Stand Luxury Stroller by Baby Trend (available from the Perfectly Safe Catalog, 800-837-KIDS). This one has a canopied, reclining seat for baby, all-terrain wheels, and a large storage basket beneath. Behind baby's spot is a padded seat, plus a platform if the toddler doesn't want to sit.

Maclaren double strollers are a popular, sturdy, lightweight ride for two. Just twenty-nine inches wide, they are only a few inches wider than front-to-back models, yet are much easier to maneuver, allow children to enter and exit on their own, and fold up like an umbrella stroller for travel. They are distributed in the United States by KidCo (901 E. Orchard Ave., Building E, Mundelein, IL, 60060-3016; 800-553-5529; KidCoEmail@aol.com).

An alternative to the double stroller is a pair of simple six-inch spacer bars that connect two umbrella strollers easily: Connect Two from Two By Two (800-526-2594 for info, or order from the Kids Club catalog, 800-363-0500) fits any lightweight stroller no matter the shape or size, and disconnects as fast as you can say, "No, Mommy, *you* push me!"

CITY KIDS

Whether you live in a big city or are planning on visiting one, maneuvering two or more kids and their many accessories through crowded streets, traffic, and subways is practically an extreme sport. Some of the urban athletes who attempt this on a daily basis offer this advice:

- Look for sturdy yet lightweight strollers. Umbrella strollers are best for logging miles on city streets and for packing into taxis or lugging in three-story walk-ups. One of the best-made lightweight strollers is from the English manufacturer Maclaren (available from KidCo, 800-553-5529); pricey but made for serious strolling.

- Carry the baby in a sling or front carrier and let the older child ride in a stroller.

- Keep a close watch on children when walking or even standing on city streets. They can wander off the curb and into harm's way in a split second.

- Don't use a stroller on or near a subway; always fold it and carry or walk with the older child, and use a sling or backpack for the baby. According to the New York Metropolitan Transit Authority, in New York alone, an average of one child per month is seriously injured when open strollers and subway travel mix. Most accidents occur when children are carried up and down stairs or escalators while in their strollers; however, strollers can get caught in subway doors and may be dragged by the train. Since subway platforms slope slightly for water drainage, unattended strollers can roll onto the tracks.

Sleeping Stuff

If you are in the habit of listening to your firstborn sleep through a baby monitor, you may be wondering what will happen when you have a newborn to tune in to as well. If you can wean yourself from monitoring your older child, by all means, take the jump.

If the older child still requires monitoring, or if the children's bedrooms are far apart or on different floors, you will require two setups. You may avoid potential static problems by purchasing two sets from the same manufacturer—make sure that they have at least two channels in case of interference.

Feeding Time

Although you'll need to restock bottle nipples and pacifiers (which can get enlarged, sticky, and worn), it's fine to reuse your first child's bibs, cups, and utensils for your second child. But it's a wise idea to have a few new items on hand to steer clear of jealousy. Your four-year-old might have been bib-free for years but disintegrate into tears when you give her favorite Barney bib to the new baby. Buy a couple of new ones just for the infant, and work on making the hand-me-downs the sibling's area. ("Hey, you don't use this anymore. Is there anyone else who might be able to wear this at mealtime?")

Carry-Alls

You won't need a U-Haul to cart around two children's accouterments. In fact, June found herself toting much *less* gear when she had two kids, two years apart. "For one thing, they amuse each other—hence, I need fewer toys and distractions." An extra-large diaper bag or a backpack with lots of nooks and crannies will fill the bill. Many parents swear by the Lands' End (800-356-4444) diaper bag. It's big enough for both kids' stuff and has lots of pockets and pouches for incidentals.

If your children have differing schedules, you may consider having three bags at the ready: one just for the older child (for day care or dance class), one just for the baby, and one for both of them together. It may sound like overkill, but if you are constantly taking changes of clothes or diapers in and out of one bag, this tactic makes a lot of sense.

Active Accessories

Sporty types will find several options for taking two kids on the go. Bicyclists can use a trailer for two such as the models from Burley (800-311-5294; http://www.burley.com), CycleTote (800-747-2407; http://www.cycletote.com), and Kiddie Kart Trailers (800-967-4307). Like a handful of models, the Duosport (Kids Club catalog, 800-363-0500) converts from bicycle trailer to stroller in seconds and comes with canopy, roll bar, rear and side reflectors, safety flat, and rain shield. The helpful Internet document "Bike Trailers" at http://danenet.wicip.org/bcp/bike____trailers.html provides a summary of products, safety tips, and recommendations amassed from Usenet postings.

If running is more your speed, there are jogging strollers designed for two or even three kids. Contact Racing Strollers (800-241-1848), Runabout (800-832-2376), and CycleTote (800-747-2407) for brochures.

Childproofing Redux

When a new baby comes along, your first child's high chair, crib, stroller, playpen, and the like get a second chance. Before you strap baby in, however, do a thorough check to ensure these items are as safe as you remember them: Look for peeling paint or chipped, cracked plastic. Make sure that all bolts, latches, and hardware are secure. Safety belts or harnesses should be in good shape. A thorough washing will freshen fabric covers or seats and may remove potential allergens.

Even the most safety-conscious first-time parents have

a way of becoming less diligent in that department as their baby turns into a toddler or preschooler. In fact, many of these are intentional shifts: The gate comes down so the toddler can come and go as he pleases; potty lock comes off during toilet learning; games or products with small parts are placed on the lowest tables or an accessible toy shelf.

Go through your house on all fours and look for exposed outlets, drapery cords, extension cords, cables, wires, anything that a baby could wrap himself up in or pull down. And check your firstborn's scattered toys and items carefully. Watch for loose, removable, or small parts; products with long strings; sharp-edged items; and sponges, art supplies, crafts, and paper products that might end up in the wrong hands (or mouth). Enlist your older child's help with this search and teach him how to keep his sibling safe. Even my three-year-old knows to ask, "Is this too small for Josh to play with?"

Susan Baril of the Catalog for Safe Beginnings (800-598-8911) suggests these tips for parents of two:

- Install a safety gate at the entrance to your older child's room. It can prevent injuries and also gives the firstborn a space of her own. The baby can still see into the room and not feel isolated.

- A "Cozy Crib Tent," a protective netting attached with Velcro over the top of the crib, helps keep baby safe from a toddler's urge to throw toys into the crib to comfort a crying baby. (It keeps pets from joining baby, too.)

- If you wonder about any of your older child's toys, keep a small-object tester (about the size of a film canister) on hand to check when needed.

- Use a play yard (or portable crib) or gate off a space just for your older child. He or she can have a special activity area for toys with small parts that's safe from baby. And your little one won't feel totally left out—

he or she can still see what's going on inside. Make a special play time for your older child during baby's nap. When baby's asleep, he can take out the toys that are not safe for baby.

Take some time with a safety-product catalog like Safe Beginnings or Perfectly Safe (800-837-KIDS) to get an idea of the latest, most innovative ideas in childproofing. Indeed, products that were considered on the cutting edge several years ago may have already been replaced by newer, smarter solutions.

Shop at Home

Sometimes a trip to the mall can be a welcome outing for housebound parents or a warm (or air-conditioned) retreat during seasonal extremes. Still, keeping two or more kids amused while shopping is a feat best achieved when the planets are aligned just so.

Mail-order catalogs are a celestial alternative. You can send for just about anything—great children's products, housewares, bedding, health and safety items, crafts, and more—without ever leaving your glider rocker. Here are some favorites for busy families:

Children's Clothing

- After the Stork (800-441-4775; http://www.afterthe stork.com; storkmail@afterthestork.com): colorful, all-cotton onesies, overalls, coveralls, footed pants, leggings, and other basics for babies and toddlers. Lots of essentials for older kids, too, including shoes, belts, sweats, and outerwear.

- Biobottoms (800-766-1254; http://www.biobottoms. com; children@biobottoms.com): bright, natural-fiber clothing and outerwear for babies, toddlers, and older kids—coveralls, onesies, pants, overalls, tees, and turtlenecks in 100 percent cotton. Also a great source for natural diapering products, featuring Biobottoms and Cottonbottoms cotton diapers and accessories.

- Hanna Andersson (800-222-0544; http://www.hanna Andersson.com): durable, colorful clothes made from soft Swedish cotton for babies through adults.

- Lands' End Kids' Catalog (800-356-4444): the same high-quality fabrics and designs you've seen in the adult catalog, but kid-sized. Also cotton flannel crib ensembles, backpacks, school packs, and some of the toughest, roomiest diaper bags around.

- Patagonia Kids (800-336-9090: http://www.patagonia. com/): extreme clothing for the outdoors, for all ages—flannel and winter linen coveralls, quilted jackets, fleece booties and mittens, and the ultracozy Baby Shapka Bunting (converts to zippered legs for wear in car seats and backpacks).

- Playclothes (800-362-7529; http://www.playclothes. com): fun active wear, mostly for toddlers (size 2T) on up.

- Warner Bros. Studio Store Catalog (800-223-6524): Your child will sing a Looney Tune when you dress him in 100 percent cotton sweats and overalls emblazoned with his favorite Warner Bros. characters (lots for grown-ups, too). The gang shows up on jewelry, housewares, and decorative items as well.

Children's Products

- AVON (800-FOR-AVON; http://www.avon.com): As you might expect, there are plenty of makeup items, fragrances, and seasonal gifts (and for busy parents, this is a great way to shop), but now there are also pages of kids' items, such as bath-time products, children's books, craft kits, videos, and audiocassettes. Call for a free catalog.

- The Baby Catalog of America (800-752-9736; http://www.toto.com/bca; bca@toto.com): features nursery items, feeding products, bath and potty needs, health and safety devices, books and videotapes, and special gifts.

- The Catalog for Safe Beginnings (800-598-8911; http://www.safebeginnings.com): features nursery accessories, baby-proofing basics, diaper bags and baby carriers, feeding and nursing accessories, play pads, activity centers, exercisers, outdoor gear including bike seats, helmets, and clothing, and parenting books and videos. Free catalog also includes safety tips for the home.

- Community Playthings (800-777-4244; http://www.bruderhof.com/): Families of two or more children, particularly small children, can find innovative furniture and exceptionally durable wood toys in this catalog. A great resource for solid maple play centers, chairs, high chairs, cribs, kid-size tables, bookshelves, "kitchens," and indoor play equipment (gyms and "toddler towns").

- Ecobaby (800-596-7450; http://www.ecobaby.com): a full line of natural products for babies and young children. Shop for diapering products, baby slings, organic cotton and natural-fiber clothing, natural bedding, futons, wood toys and furniture, nursing bras and accessories, homeopathic remedies, and many other items.

- Hand in Hand (800-872-9745): a carefully selected collection of traditional and innovative products for children's early years, such as kid-size furniture, bath toys, musical instruments, art supplies, videos, books, housewares, and safety and travel products. Free catalog.

- J.C. Penney (800-222-6161; http//www.jcpenney.com/): In addition to J.C. Penney's main catalog, there are smaller, specialized mail-order catalogs just for expectant mothers and new babies. Call for free catalogs offering maternity wear, baby furniture, car seats and strollers, safety items, infant and toddler clothing, and the like.

- Kids Club (800-363-0500): A shopper's club for the catalog set, Kids Club items sell at about 40 to 60 percent off other mail-order companies, and sometimes even less. Great for feeding accessories, nursery needs, bath items, strollers, safety products, toys. Have one on hand for price comparisons. (Ordering is usually worth the nominal "membership" fee; there's no charge for a catalog.)

- Natural Resources (800-557-2229): a free catalog from the operators of Natural Resources, a pregnancy, childbirth, and early parenting resource center located in San Francisco. They make an effort to provide environmentally conscious, cruelty-free products, such as diapering supplies; herbal teas and vitamins; books on pregnancy, childbirth, motherhood, breast-feeding, baby nutrition, fatherhood, and homeopathy and herbs; audiotapes for relaxation; baby carriers, and other accessories.

- One Step Ahead (800-274-8440): products for babies, toddlers, and young children, with a special emphasis on those first few months. Look for bedding, feeding-time necessities, toy-storage ideas, baby-proofing basics, even breast-feeding accessories for Mom. Free catalog.

- Perfectly Safe Catalog (800-837-KIDS): hundreds of exclusive and innovative home, auto, fire and other safety items; plus strollers, toys, books, feeding supplies, and hard-to-find products for home, outdoors, travel, and playtime.

- The Right Start Catalog (800-548-8531): a rich resource for nursery and feeding basics as well as innovative, problem-solving products. Free catalog.

- Spiegel (800-345-4500; http://www.spiegel.com/): Shop for cribs, strollers, high chairs, nursery monitors, and the like; linens, blankets, curtains, and throws for the nursery; and kid-size furniture such as toddler beds, dressers, bookshelves, personalized step stools, and toy chests. There's a small fee for the catalog, but in most cases it can be credited toward a merchandise certificate; ask for details.

Toys, Games, Music

- Alcazar Music (800-541-9904): specializes in independent-label and hard-to-find releases; offers an outstanding selection, from folk and classical music and to children's books on tape. Contact for extensive catalog. (There's a fee for the catalog, but it will be credited toward your first purchase.)

- Animal Town (800-445-8642): not so much animals, but fun, stimulating, and practical toys and books for kids. Animal Town seeks out products that are easy to understand and use, nonviolent, meaningful, culturally diverse, durable, fairly priced, and created mainly from renewable resources (wood, cotton, or paper). Free catalog.

- Back to Basics Toys (800-356-5360): classic, high-quality, long-lasting toys that encourage creativity, expand young minds, and promote physical development. Free catalog.

- Childcraft (800-631-5657): Kids get crafty with Childcraft's traditional hardwood blocks; construction sets; plastic mini menageries from the wild, the farm, and under the sea; easels, messy mats, and washable tempera paints; and much more, from microscopes to sporting goods. Free catalog.

- Constructive Playthings (800-832-0572): toys fostering

creativity, imagination, and developmental growth. Free catalog.

- Discovery Toys (800-426-4777): Not a catalog company, Discovery Toys are sold through independent consultants, usually through demonstration "parties." But these high-quality toys and books are worth going out of your way for. There's an excellent selection of fun, durable, sensory-stimulating infant and toddler items and much more for older kids, including clothing. Call for a catalog and the name of your local consultant.

- Dover Publications (31 East 2nd Street, Mineola, NY 11501): a must for parents looking for ways to entertain toddlers or older children (while the baby nurses, perhaps?). Here they'll find storybooks, coloring books, activity books, stickers, paper dolls, stencil books, posters, and classics at extraordinary prices. (Little activity books cost one dollar; most other books are less than four dollars.) Write for a free catalog.

- The Great Kids Company (800-533-2166): Items for babies and toddlers include interactive fun centers, shape sorters, classic wooden alphabet blocks, discovery and activity centers, and bath-time toys. A big selection of arts and crafts items for kids over age three. Plus small-scale furniture, science and nature kits, and outdoor fun. Free catalog.

- HearthSong (800-325-2502): an intriguing selection of toys and games with multicultural influences, including crafts, games, books, jewelry and science kits, outdoor toys, kites, and more. Free catalog.

- Lily's Kids (800-285-5555): Aimed mostly at the over-three crowd, this catalog has several fun and educational items for little ones, such as a bright and busy personalized activity mat for babies; squeezy-soft fabric-covered foam blocks and nesting learning blocks; cotton/canvas busy books; and colorful wooden stacking rings. Free catalog.

- Oriental Trading Company (800-228-2269; http://www.oriental.com): My favorite catalog for party favors (many of the items within are sold in bulk), this features a wacky assortment of gifts, party supplies, toys, and knickknacks, not only for kids, at terrific prices. Free catalog.

- Sensational Beginnings (800-444-2147): unique and innovative toys, crafts, and projects for kids of all ages. Free catalog.

- Toys to Grow On (800-542-8338): The emphasis here is on crafts and imaginative play, with great prices and comprehensive play sets, mostly for kids over age four. Free catalog.

- Troll Learn & Play (800-247-6106): educational puzzles and games, art supplies, active toys, personalized bags and furniture, books and videos. Free catalog.

Books: For Children and Parents

- Amazon.com (http://www.amazon.com): Save up to 40 percent on books every day at "the Earth's largest bookstore." They'll try their best to locate virtually any book you request, even if it's out of print or hard to find. This web site offers reviews and book excerpts, plus they will send e-mail notices about new releases from the authors you love or on the topics of your choice.

- The Book Lady (800-766-7323; www.booklady.com/): a descriptive catalog of children's books and resources designed for teachers, but invaluable to parents.

- Chinaberry Book Service (800-776-2242): a free, highly descriptive catalog to guide you through the maze of children's books available today. Books are organized by levels, not ages, and each book has been hand-picked for its uniqueness. Also, older children's literature, crafts books, parenting titles, family music and stories on tape, and a small selection of aromatherapy products.

- **Imprints (503-371-4445):** Birth & Life Bookstore's free catalog of books, pamphlets, and video and audio recordings focusing on pregnancy, childbirth, breastfeeding, child care and development, midwifery, parenthood, postpartum adjustment, nutrition, women's health, and other topics.

Bed and Bath

- **Coming Home (800-345-3696):** Lands' End's collection of sheets, blankets, comforters, mattress pads, and quilts include items for baby's room too.

- **The Company Store (800-285-3696):** a family-size assortment of sheets, quilts, blankets, down comforters, and a unique assortment of odd-shaped pillows (great for pregnancy).

- **Garnet Hill (800-622-6216):** exquisite natural-fiber bedding, blankets, and quilts, among other cozies.

And You Are . . . ?

"Kimmy is a high-needs baby, and Lucas is adjusting to a lot of changes, including growing up," Ashleigh sighs. "There is a lot of stress at home, and this has had a negative effect on our relationship. We both resent the amount of work we each have and the lack of help and understanding from each other. We both have commented that it seems like we are living our own separate lives."

There is a lot of attention to be lavished in a household of two or more children, from the moment the first one wakes up until the last one is tucked into bed. As we've discussed, the you-take-him-I'll-take-her approach means that both kids get some alone time with parents. It also helps Mom and Dad get things done so that no one is left washing dishes during *The Late Show*.

Unfortunately, this means that even when both you and your partner are at home, you may scarcely see one another. There will most likely be household or personal details to attend to once the kids have drifted off. And when you are finally alone and in the same room, you both may need to unplug and unwind more than anything else. Let's see, an episode of *Seinfeld* or an examination of our relationship and our life goals? Tough choice.

Is this the end of intimacy as we know it? Family life, as loving as it can be, does take a toll on tenderness if you don't work at it. This doesn't mean you are required to hire a sitter every week or feel pressure to discuss your deepest thoughts when the dust finally settles at 10:00 P.M. After all, working at your relationship shouldn't become just another chore after laundry and clipping the dog's nails. There are subtle ways to stoke the embers of your relationship, and you don't need to quit your job or send your kids away to feed the fire.

Here and Now

These days are trying, frustrating, and not always rewarding. Nevertheless, they are fleeting, says Renée, mother of three. "We get through the tough times by acknowledging that yes, this is the most exhausted we will probably ever be in our lives, but it won't last long. Soon they'll be out the door, even though it doesn't feel that way now!"

Realizing that this chaotic stage is temporary can get you through, but only if you share this vision. A parent who chooses to sulk or complain about today's missed opportunities can't work effectively with a partner who has come to terms with what needs to be done. "The more kids you add, the more things you have to do, the more schedules you have to juggle—it's that simple," says Jennifer. "As our children are still young, we don't have a lot of time out alone together. We try to make the most of any special opportunity we get to be together without the kids. But our family is what is most important now. You learn to make the most of quiet moments, and you learn to talk fast!"

Talking—whatever speed—is the key to a family's health and future. It's important to think of yourselves as a team working on a common project, a start-up venture if you will. Your product? A robust, loving family. As with any project, life's petty annoyances have the potential to gunk up the work flow. Unless these small problems are dealt with properly, they tend to grow large and troublesome, tipping the scales. Feelings get hurt, and generally there's a lot less smiling going on.

To avoid misunderstandings, Alyson and her husband make an effort to listen and stay in tune with each other. "We really respect each other's feelings, attitudes, and rules," she says. "We do the same bedtime ritual every night so that there is no confusion. We respect what each other does during the day and all we do in the evening. We try to talk on the phone during each day to keep the other up on activities." With three kids, they make every effort to get out alone together regularly. "We *always* go out together on the weekends, except due to illness or something. We even hire two baby-sitters for the same night because of the baby."

As Alyson demonstrates, keeping the lines of communication open between you and your partner is critical to the success of your "venture," especially as a parent of two or more. Fortunately, communicating can be easier going from one child to two than when you had your first child. "When you have your first, aside from dealing with a newborn, you take on new roles with each other as parents and partners," she continues. "That can be tough on a marriage because you do not know how to act with each other. After your second or third is born, however, your roles are already clear. Communicating is much less complicated."

Ultimately, the challenges of parenting two can enrich and reinforce a partnership. "I think that although it has been a frustrating first year with our second, it has really strengthened our marriage," says Lauren. "The tough times have brought us closer, I guess, because we are in this together. We realized that we need each other to lean on when times get hard. We learned to work with, rather than against, each other. We know now that we love each other more than ever."

Finding Time When There Isn't Any

With so much to do away from the home and inside of it, the lines of communication can quickly deteriorate to a suite of rote questions and responses and little meaningful interaction. Early attempts at "grown-up" conversations around the dinner table can scare parents off in a matter of a few meals. Even the most sensitive, open couples lose their determination when a six-year-old tries too hard to chime in. "If we can finish a conversation in one sitting, it's amazing," says Jennifer.

When parents' dialogues deteriorate, so can their affectionate feelings for each other. It's quite common for couples tending to several children to fall into a rut of breakfast, work, dinner, baths, and bedtime. Not that any of this is particularly *bad*—but it could be better.

This calls for some serious relationship recharging. And that starts with being alone regularly. Finding time alone with your partner isn't a selfish or neglectful thing to do to your kids. If anything, it's a healthy goal to have. Getting out socially rejuices your soul and refreshes your perspective. It gives you the chance to remember all the things you love about each other, which in turn boosts your self-esteem—and that makes you a better parent.

Research has also shown that children fare better when parents are in a loving, warm relationship—no surprises there. In fact, parents' interactions with each other can have a profound effect on how siblings treat each other. So being loving and attentive with your spouse can make for a happier family all around.

Look for quiet opportunities to spend time together, whether that means twenty minutes after the kids are asleep or a more elaborate evening out. If time for the two of you seems truly elusive, you'll need to find creative ways to let the other know you still care. Some solutions:

- Pay attention to each other. If your partner is trying to tell you something meaningful, but the children keep interrupting, put if off until they are in bed.

- Once a week, give the kids an early dinner and arrange a more romantic menu for after they're asleep. (Romantic can be simple: Candles and some soft music can *transform* spaghetti and garlic bread.)

- Hire a sitter regularly, if only for an hour or two. Go out for coffee and dessert.

- If you must sit in front of the television, hold hands and cuddle.

- Don't forget special occasions, even the silly ones. You don't have to go to a fancy restaurant to commemorate your first kiss, but don't let the day end without planting one in remembrance.

- Have lunch together at least once a month if possible. Sitters aren't just for evenings, you know.

- Enforce nap times and bedtimes.

- Sitters are also handy on weekend mornings or afternoons. Go out for breakfast or Sunday brunch; take in a matinee or play golf.

- Praise each other's parenting skills; criticize thoughtfully.

- Sign up for a course together—massage, ballroom dancing. You'll be assured of together time each week.

- Get season tickets to sporting or cultural events; for instance, a summer theater series. Line up sitters *now.*

- Make sure you give each other some time alone each week.

LOCATING A BABYSITTER

Hiring a sitter for your children is not cruel or neglectful, and does not in any way make you a bad parent. On the other hand, feeling overwhelmed, exhausted, and lonely, or resenting the time you can't spend with your partner, isn't doing anyone any good. Putting effort and affection into your relationship will have positive effects on the whole family, I assure you.

If you don't have a regular sitter, start looking for one! It may take a while to find an individual whom you can trust, and the best ones get booked up quickly.

- Ask neighbors with small children for sitter recommendations; ask neighbors with older children whether their kids are interested in sitting.

- Find out if day-care staff members would be available.

- Check church or synagogue postings or ask fellow worshipers.

- Place an ad in your community newspaper. Be specific about your requirements.

- Look in your pediatrician's office or call your local hospital for referrals.

- At your next play-group meeting, see if any other parents would be interested in care-swapping.

- Think about hiring two sitters simultaneously for one-on-one care.

- Ask your own parents and siblings!

The Romance Department

"As for your sex life, it all goes downhill after having a second baby . . . at least for a while, anyway," says Michelle. "You are just *too tired*. And even when you don't have the late nights awake with the baby, you are so exhausted from 'loving' all day that you just don't want to do it anymore! You just want to sleep because you know that tomorrow brings more of the same."

Intimacy is important, as important to your relationship as sleep, as a matter of fact. Though given the choice at 11:00 P.M., many harried parents will choose shut-eye over sex. And that's a shame, because intimacy in all its forms—touching, cuddling, making love—can strengthen your relationship and improve your mood.

The idea of a major sex-life overhaul may seem daunting, even laughable at this time. So give yourselves a break. But don't feel so pressured by what you think you should be "doing" that you avoid each other completely. After all, the earth needn't move for the two of you to shake up your relationship. So why not start with a few sweet, simple gestures that can fuel the fire a bit?

- Exercise regularly. You'll feel better about your body and have more energy for *other* pursuits.

- Read a romantic novel to each other.

- Be a great parent. (Says Renée, "There is no stronger aphrodisiac than witnessing the intense love my husband has for his kids.")

- Hide a suggestive love note in your partner's briefcase, or send him a tantalizing E-mail.

- Take the kids for a stroll and hold your partner's hand.

- Put on some quiet music and slow-dance in the living room.

- Have lunch together. (Interpret that as you wish.)

- Arrange an overnight getaway—you don't have to go far.

- Turn off the television.

Time for Yourself

To be loved, you must first love yourself, or so they say. "They" have a point. Taking some time each week to focus on yourself—without the kids, without your partner—gives you the chance to relax and rejuvenate, to devote some time purely to you. When you pamper yourself a bit, you feel special, attractive, loved. And all the more equipped to love someone else.

An obvious activity for this private time is exercise of some sort. You'll feel better and be better able to handle unruly children if you work out on a regular basis. Ideally, some form of exercise should be a daily activity—whether it's walking the dog, swimming at lunch, taking a bike ride before the children wake up. If you can, use this stolen time for something special. Like exercise, doing something seriously fun or shamefully indulgent at least once a week will boost your spirits as well. Just make sure it's something you purely enjoy. No guilt, no calorie counting, no shopping for milk allowed (unless it's an emergency).

If you can swing an hour or two of on-your-own time, try these suggestions:

- Do something quietly creative: pottery, photography, sketching. Think about how much your child enjoys the fun and freedom of arts and crafts. And like your child, don't make too much of an effort to stay clean.

- Take a class in t'ai chi or yoga—focusing on something other than children, deadlines, and housework for even an hour a week will refresh your mind and soothe your soul.

- Enroll in a dance class for fun and exercise. Tap your troubles away!

- Take a relaxing bath. Lock the door.

- Spend two hours in a bookstore just browsing. Pick up magazines that you would never consider buying. This escape is particularly effective if you can find a shop with overstuffed chairs and a coffee bar.

- Get a manicure, pedicure, facial, or a massage.

- Take the cordless phone, settle into a quiet place, and call an old friend who makes you laugh.

No one will give you a parenting demerit for stealing some time for yourselves—no one but you, that is. Focusing on each other rather than on what needs to be fixed, the stray crayon marks on the wall, or who washed out the bottles last—at least every now and then—will do wonders for your relationship and have no lasting effect on your living environment. Your children will forgive you, too, although they won't advertise that fact.

Just as good parenting takes a lot of effort and attention, so does maintaining a positive, loving relationship. And what better environment for your children than a home grounded by a strong marriage or partnership. Everybody wins!

Becoming a Family

"One day, out of nowhere, Hannah said, 'Mom, thank you for having Isaac,'" Renée remembers. "I was so taken aback that a four-year-old would say such a thing that I replied, 'What do you mean? Why are you thanking me?' She said, 'Because he's so cute and I love him so much. And now I can always have someone to play with.' I was so choked up. It's this big cliché that a sibling is the greatest gift you can give your child, and here I was lucky enough to be living it."

Togetherness. Support. Unconditional love. There's so much more to being a part of a family than "coping" or "managing" its members. Clearly it can seem that just getting through the day with everyone healthy and fed, and with as few meltdowns as possible, is the best you can hope for with two young children. And in the early days, making it through is reward enough.

Once all of your family members get used to the idea that baby's here to stay, you can focus on nurturing and strengthening the bonds you share. How quickly you all move into this next stage depends on how accepting you, your partner, and older child have been of the changes in your lives and the adjustments you've had to make. It also depends on the support you give your older child as he figures out his new role.

It may take months until you all feel like a family, or you may get that sensation as soon as you bring baby home. Mothers may feel connected to their new baby right away, but slightly estranged from their firstborn. Dads may discover newfound feelings for the older child as they spend more time together in those early days; however, they may not feel they have adequate opportunities to bond with their new baby. Siblings may find themselves struggling with a busload of unfamiliar emotions they simply can't put into words.

Now begins the work of becoming a family.

Smoothing and Soothing

It was one of those evenings when I was on my own with the two kids, then ages two and three quarters, and four and a half months. Joshua was enjoying his nightly crying jag; Sara was getting along fairly well with her fish sticks. I was bouncing Josh on my lap trying to get something in my own stomach when Sara demanded, "I want to go on your lap."

"Sara, I'm holding Josh right now and trying to eat. I can't pick you up. I'm sorry."

"I want to go on your lap," she whined.

Since Josh was crying anyway, whether on my lap or on the floor with his toys, I decided to put him down on his quilt in the other room. On my way back, I heard Sara say quietly, "I was here first."

"What did you say?"

"I was here first," she repeated softly.

"You were where first?"

"In your lap."

Aside from two solid weeks of constant tantrums when Josh first came home, this was the first time I ever heard

Sara acknowledge the hurt she was feeling, as best a toddler could. I was surprised and saddened by her remark.
In a way it was a relief to hear her acknowledge a feeling
rather than bottle it up. But of course, it was very hard
to hear.

I thought I was handling the situation quite well with
those fish sticks. But was Sara thinking, "Hey, great fish
sticks!"? Of course not. We were both preoccupied with
Josh's crying and what it meant to our time together. To
Sara, my persistent attempts to calm him down didn't
mean I was trying to have a quieter meal with her, she
was afraid that I cared more about him or that I didn't
love her as much as I used to. Unfortunately, I didn't
know this until she said something.

Since we can't read their little minds, and because many
young children can't put their thoughts into words as Sara
did, it's important to start giving children the tools they
need to identify their feelings as early as you can. Instead
of telling a withdrawn child to "cheer up," ask him if
he's feeling sad, angry, or just tired. Identify your own
emotions as they occur and explain why you feel a certain
way. A great book for introducing the concepts of moods
and emotions is *My Many Colored Days,* by Dr. Seuss (Al-
fred A. Knopf, 1996). Although a child may not be able
to recognize his feelings until age three or later, you will
be demonstrating that all of his feelings are okay and that
you'll love him regardless of his moods.

Still, the inside of a child's head can be a scary, unsettling place. You can help calm the fears and anxieties with
frequent reminders of his worth in the family and the love
that surrounds him:

- Start the day with a smile and a hug, no matter the
  weather, how much sleep you got, or how many meet-
  ings lie ahead that day.

- Sneak a special message or a favorite sticker into her
  lunch box now and then.

- Make sure she senses how much the baby loves having a big brother or sister. Point out the times she makes the baby laugh or smile when no one else can. Note the way he watches her across the room, or tries to imitate her or get her attention.

• Say "I love you" often, for no particular reason.

• Remember how little she is. Next to a baby, even a two-year-old seems like a "big kid." Don't scold her for acting her age; help her to grow at her own pace.

Apples and Oranges

One of the goals in growing a healthy, happy family is allowing each child to mature at his own pace, in his own way. This can be quite an effort for parents who expect a baby to develop in his sister or brother's footsteps. For example, as your new baby begins to work her way through her first-year milestones, you may feel tempted to compare her to her older sibling, panicking that she isn't rolling over at the same age her brother started, or happily surprised that she spared you the twelve weeks of colic that her brother suffered through.

Do yourself a favor and let her be herself. She may share some DNA and a couple of grown-ups with her sibling, but in terms of personality and physical abilities, she's on her own. For the most part, genetics will dictate when she will roll over or take those first unsteady steps. Realizing that your children are wholly separate individuals may save you some developmental worries and allow you to enjoy each child's uniqueness.

The same goes for your baby's emerging personality. Don't expect her to be quiet and unaffectionate just because her older sibling isn't a big hugging fan. Lavish her with affection unless she pushes you away too. On the other hand, if your firstborn thrives on social contact, don't force the younger child into such situations if it makes her uneasy.

"Stephanie was quicker at learning new things. She said 'mama' at four months and knew what it meant. She walked at ten months, and was talking at twelve," Connie says. Baby Joshua was in less of a rush: "He said 'mama' at seven and a half months and walked just over a year. Stephanie is the loving, caring, and cheerful type; Joshua, so far, is stubborn and very temperamental, constantly screaming for everything. Stephanie is also very creative and sensitive. Joshua would rather beat up on someone right now."

Ashleigh also sees definite differences in her children. "Lucas babbled more than Kimmy does. We've decided that he's going to be the intellect and she's going to be the daredevil. He already knows all of his letters and loves books; she just wants to go! She's very intense—a 'demanding' baby—and he is mostly laid back."

Ironically, a second-born may push herself harder, even without your prompting. Many younger siblings seem eager to keep up with their older sibling (or should I say "idol"), even if they don't seem developmentally ready. You may notice her trying to walk earlier than her brother did, or attempting athletic feats months beyond her abilities. On vacation last year, my husband and I watched in amazement as an almost-two-year-old flung herself into the grown-up swimming pool, dog-paddling vigorously to keep up with her four-year-old swimming sister. Our Sara, a bit older than the daredevil, was wading in the kiddie pool sheepishly. "She has to do everything her sister does," the parents said proudly.

It's true that the older child takes on a teaching role with the younger, even if he doesn't realize it. By just going about his business, he conveys the importance of being independent, listening to Mom and Dad, using the potty, making friends. For this reason, younger children may learn to talk, to share, even to use the potty earlier than they might have.

Then again, the overly solicitous firstborn may have the

opposite effect on his adoring sibling. It is quite common for a second-born to bask in the attention and servitude of the older child, allowing him to fetch her toys while she sits, watches, and listens. She may then put off crawling or walking, even talking. Parents may contribute to the delay by spending less time talking with the second child. They may miss opportunities for the infant to practice gross motor skills by putting him or her in a stroller or play yard while they tend to a wilder sibling.

SPECIAL-NEEDS SIBLINGS

No one expects his or her new baby to have a birth defect or a disabling illness. So when that is the case, families may have no idea where to turn for help, support, and information. My husband and I experienced this pain and frustration firsthand when our second child was born with a metabolic disease that affected his heart. We were frightened, disappointed, and bewildered. What's more, we had another child with an endless supply of questions. Not knowing the answers ourselves, we weren't sure what to tell her.

To respond to your child's questions, and to begin the slow process of education, acceptance, and coping, it is imperative that families of children with special needs connect with organizations that can help. The groups that follow can supply publications, information, and in some cases help you network with other families who can share their own stories.

And when you do find your answers, try not to overload your child with too much information. Respond to his questions truthfully, but don't go into so much detail that he becomes confused. Age-appropriate books can help: Woodbine House (6510 Bells Mill Road, Bethesda, MD 20817; 800-843-7323 or 301-897-3570) publishes a collection of children's books and resources that deal with special-needs subjects such as attention-deficit disorder, autism, cerebral palsy, Down's syndrome, mental retardation, spina bifida, and other physical and mental disabilities.

For disease or disability-specific resources, contact:

- Alliance of Genetic Support Groups: 35 Wisconsin Circle, Suite 440, Chevy Chase, MD 20815; 800-336-4363 or 301-652-5553; alliance@capaccess.org

- American Foundation for the Blind: 11 Penn Plaza, Suite 300, New York, NY 10001; 800-232-5463; 212-502-7600; http://www.afb.org/; afbinfo@afb.org

- Autism Society of America: 7910 Woodmont Avenue, Suite 650, Bethesda, MD 20814; 800-3AUTISM or 301-657-0881; http://www.autism-society.org/

- Blind Children's Center: 4120 Marathon Street, Los Angeles, CA 90029; 800-222-3566; in California, 800-222-3567 or 213-664-2153; http://www3.primenet.com/bcc/

- Cleft Palate Foundation: 1218 Grandview Avenue, Pittsburgh, PA 15211; 800-242-5338 or 412-481-1376

- CHASER (Congenital Heart Anomalies Support, Education, and Resources): 2112 North Wilkins Road, Swanton, OH 43558; 419-825-5575; myer106w@wonder.em.cdc.gov or 75050.2742@compuserve.com

- Cystic Fibrosis Foundation: 6931 Arlington Road, Bethesda, MD 20814; 800-FIGHT-CF or 301-951-4422; http://www.cff.org/; info@cff.org

- Deafness Research Foundation: 15 West 39th Street, New York, NY 10018; 212-768-1181 (voice/TTY); http://village.ios.com/~dr1/index.html; dr1@village.ios.com

- Epilepsy Foundation of America: 4351 Garden City Drive, Landover, MD 20785; 800-EFA-1000; 301-459-3700; http://www.efa.org/

- ERIC Clearinghouse on Handicapped and Gifted Education: The Council for Exceptional Children, 1920 Association Drive, Reston, VA 20191; 800-328-0272 (voice); 703-264-9449 (TTY); http://www.cec.sped.org/ericec.htm; ericec@cec.sped.org

- Muscular Dystrophy Association: 3300 East Sunrise Drive, Tucson, AZ 85718-3208; 800-572-1717 or 520-529-2000

- National Down Syndrome Society: 666 Broadway, 8th Floor, New York, NY 10012-2317; 800-221-4602 or 212-460-9330; http://www.ndss.org; info@ndss.org

- National Information Center for Children and Youth with Disabilities: PO Box 1492, Washington, DC 20013-1492; 800-695-0285 (voice/TTY) or 202-884-8200 (voice/TTY); http://www.nichcy.org; nichcy@aed.org

- National Information Center on Deafness: Gallaudet University, 800 Florida Avenue NE, Washington, DC 20002-3695; 202-651-5051; 202-651-5052 (TTY); http://www.gallaudet.edu/~nicd/; nicd@gallux.gallaudet.edu

- National Information Clearinghouse on Children Who are Deaf-Blind (DB-Link): 345 N. Monmouth Avenue, Monmouth, OR 97361; 800-438-9376; 800-854-7013 (TTY); 503-838-8776; dblink@tr.wou.edu

- National Organization for Rare Disorders: PO Box 8923, New Fairfield, CT 06812-8923; 800-999-6673 or 203-764-6518; TTY 203-746-6927; http://www.pcnet.com/~orphan/

- "Social Security and SSI Benefits for Children with Disabilities": Call 800-772-1213 to order this FREE booklet (Publication No. 05-10026) from the Social Security Administration that gives an overview of benefits available to children.

- Spina Bifida Association of America: 4590 MacArthur Boulevard NW, Suite 250, Washington, DC 20007-4226;

800-621-3141 or 202-944-3285; http://www.sbaa.org/
home.htm; sbaa@sbaa.org

- United Cerebral Palsy Associations: 1660 L Street NW,
  Suite 700, Washington, DC 20036-5602; 800-872-5827 or
  202-776-0406; http://www.ucpa.org/; ucpnatl@ucpa.
  org

- United Mitochondrial Disease Foundation: PO Box
  1151, Monroeville, PA 15146-1151; 412-856-1297; http://
  biochemgen.ucsd.edu/umdf/

Getting Over the Guilt

"I spend a good amount of my free time reading about
toddler and preschooler behavior," says Rebecca, who has
a three-year-old as well as a nine-monther. "But I rarely
pick up a book about babies. I feel like I'm ignoring my
little one."

When a new baby's coming to your house, there is a
lot of effort spent on making the first child feel important
and loved in the days before and after his sibling's arrival.
When all this energy is directed toward the firstborn, especially in the early months, it's very common for parents
to feel that the baby, not the firstborn, is the one who is
getting neglected, ignored, or "cheated" in some way.
They don't get nearly as much private time with you as
the first did. Certainly they aren't picked up or cuddled
as much as the first. When both kids are melting down,
it just seems more efficient, more worthwhile even, to
tend to the toddler.

Parents shouldn't beat themselves up about this too
much. You are most likely giving the baby enough attention, even if it doesn't feel that way. You might not rush
to his side as quickly as you did your first, but unless
you abandon him in a playpen for hours on end or com-

pletely ignore his cries of hunger or pain, you should not feel that you are neglecting him. In fact, he may learn faster than a firstborn how to be patient. Remember, too, your second-born won't feel as though he lost your undivided attention. Unlike your first, he never had you all to himself in the first place. Plus he gets plenty of smiles, hugs, and time from his big sib.

If you still think that your new baby is getting the short shrift, make a point to spend time alone with him. A couple of "sessions" spent one on one can make a big difference to both of you.

Rivalry Revisited

By about the half-year mark, you will notice a miraculous difference in the way your children relate to one another. The wrinkled, helpless infant who had little in common with his older sibling has become something resembling a playmate. His big brother can probably make him laugh just by entering the room. The baby may be sitting up so that he looks deceptively like a peer. He is also starting to go after whatever catches his eye—namely, your other child's toys.

Your older child may react in several ways (all in the same afternoon). He may begin talking to the baby more and trying to attend to his needs on his own, such as fetching the baby's toys, books, or blankie. The two may babble and giggle at each other from the car seats. And he'll probably delight in his ability to make the baby laugh.

Unfortunately, while the two are finally becoming friendly, the time is ripe for another bout of sibling rivalry. The older child may go through another phase of tantrums or negativity once the baby becomes mobile. At this age the sibling may have become used to the idea of bringing his choice of toys to the baby and watching him beam with appreciation. But suddenly this crawling, drooling little person who doesn't even understand "No" has free run of the playroom, taking and chewing as he pleases.

As Jackie illustrates: "Until recently, my daughter had no problems at all with her little brother—she basically ignored him. Now that he is a mobile creature, however, there is a turf war waging."

You can help divert these conflicts by becoming your older child's ally in preserving his belongings. Sharing is great, particularly when it's your older child's idea, but he shouldn't be expected to hand over any cherished plaything your crawling baby may deem slobber-worthy. Indeed, even a less-than-beloved plaything may suddenly soar to the top ten the second a sibling lays a paw on it. Practice the art of distraction with both. Offer special activities to the older child while the baby wanders the room. Or if the infant has commandeered a firstborn's favorite toy, quickly make a swap—the younger may be less enamored of it and just as happy to gnaw on something else.

If the older child cries or yells when the baby takes his stuff, talk to him calmly and reassure him that he doesn't have to share everything all the time. Of course, an aggressive response from your child (hitting, slapping the baby) requires immediate attention. Again, don't lose your cool, but let him know, firmly and without hesitation, that hitting is unacceptable. Give him an option besides aggression. Tell him it's okay for him to say "No" and for him to take back his toy (gently). You might also suggest that he offer something else to the baby instead, one of the baby's own toys, for instance. Your older child might surprise you and give the baby one of his favorite toys. To head off frequent struggles, try setting up an area that's either off-limits to the baby or out of his reach for the time being.

Becoming Friends

While this can be a tough time for an older sibling, it also means the two can finally start to become confidants. "At six months and nineteen months, Cody and Ben are now good friends," Jeanette says. "Cody just lights up when he sees Ben coming. And when we get around other kids and one of them gets too close to Cody, Ben has to come 'protect' him. We were baby-sitting the other day with several kids and one of them accidentally stepped on Cody's hand. Cody yelled. Ben came over and pushed the other kid away, got down and was hugging and patting Cody."

Christine's firstborn also sees a need to serve as guardian for his sibling. "At age three, my son is very protective of his baby sister when she gets her immunizations. He actually gets mad at the doctor for making his Deanna cry."

Ashleigh also saw a difference near the half-year mark. "They became friends when Kimmy started sitting up. And now that she crawls, she's all over him—she watches everything he does in fascination. When we started 'walking' her around the house, he would see her coming and smile, like he was so proud of her."

At this age they may start to enjoy simple games and being together. They might even find ways to appreciate the same toys, although they will use them differently. For instance, they can both enjoy looking at books (perhaps the older can read to the baby), stacking and building with blocks, or spending an afternoon in the sand. Says Jennifer, "My four-year-old and two-and-a-half-year-old do not play at the same level, but he is very patient with her and tries to teach her how to do things. She will bring him balls to put on his tee when he is practicing baseball."

Playing Favorites

So finally your kids have decided that they like each other after all. Then one day when you're quietly enjoying a puzzle or painting sunsets with your daughter, you may be disappointed—annoyed, even—by the sudden wail of your son waking up from his nap. At that time, a feeling so guilt-laden, so unthinkable, may prick your soul—the feeling that you'd rather be with one instead of the other. Horrors! Could you actually have a "favorite"? Don't you love them both equally with no partiality whatsoever?

Don't beat yourself up over this. It's perfectly normal to prefer to be with one child at times, particularly if he's at an age when you can converse well and enjoy a wide range of activities together. Babies can be a lot of work, physically and emotionally. Would you rather blow bubbles with a laughing four-year-old or rock a colicky newborn? Aha.

As colic becomes a distant memory and you're dealing with two distinct personalities, surely there will be aspects of each child you admire and those you dislike. Then there are moods, swayed by hunger, fatigue, jealousy, success, weather, that turn the most likable children into tiny monsters. In fact, it's entirely possible to love both children tremendously and not particularly want to be with either one at the moment! (Of course, if you feel that you are seriously neglecting one of your children for any length of time, make sure you talk to your doctor about your concerns.)

Let yourself enjoy the warm feelings you have for each child individually. Your love for them will mature as they do—but not without a fight.

Conclusion

It's 5:30 P.M. on a Tuesday evening.

We are in the backyard with all of Sara's bubble-blowing supplies laid out on her picnic table. There are trays and wands of all shapes and colors. I choose the large rings that produce bubbles as big as Sara's three-year-old body, and then some.

Josh is now nine months old. He seems eager to blow his own bubbles, but it appears that he will settle for eating the soap. From the grass, he pulls up on the picnic table and begins swiping at the red and blue wands that are scattered about. He seems bent on grabbing the silhouette of a dinosaur.

"Here, let me show you," Sara says in her proud little-helper voice. She picks up the dinosaur wand and tosses it onto the platter of bubble soap, which splashes over the sides and oozes onto the table.

"Here you go, Josh," she says with glee. Josh cackles, accepts the dinosaur wand, and lowers himself down onto his diaper. The wand goes straight into his mouth.

"No, Josh," Sara shouts, and grabs it from his hands. Giggles again. And he's up!

It has been a long year from the moment I discovered my second pregnancy to these lingering summer days.

We have made it through my son's critical illness. He's learned to roll, to crawl, to cruise, to feed himself, to put soapy wands in his mouth. Sara has made it through confusion, disappointments, tantrums, triumphs, and potty training. Now a big sister, she can almost write her name and do an arabesque.

And I have changed as well. I believe that having two kids has made me a better parent. There were hard times, there were frustrating times, but I learned to consider their tender hearts and minds before reacting to any of them. In this first year as siblings, they needed love more than scolding; attention more than time-outs. I discovered ways to put aside the anger and to appreciate their smallness. I know now to pick my fights carefully, to take deep breaths, and to hug them as many times a day as possible.

Meanwhile, the two have fallen in love with each other. There is no one who can elicit a smile from Joshua the way Sara can, simply at will. She makes him laugh by shouting the names of objects around the room: "Nose! Shoe! Door! Ball!" He cheers, croons his delight, adores her attention. Indeed, in his earliest days we doubted that we'd ever see him smile. Sara can't remember a time when he didn't.

It's time to finish making dinner, I tell Sara. She asks for more bubbles, please, without a trace of a whine or the hint of a demand. I glance at Josh, who has crawled to a thick patch of grass and seems perfectly content to watch the dog sleep in the sun. A couple more bubbles wouldn't hurt, I guess.

The sun is still strong at this time of day, but a gentle breeze makes it bearable. I wave the circular wand to create an enormous glistening bubble, which Sara chases as it rises up into the warm wind. I do a few more. As they leave my wand, they contort and warp and reflect the light until POP! The children squeal.

One more fragile bubble. In this one I can see a rainbow. It is so beautiful, so fleeting. Then as suddenly as it appeared, it is gone. I scoop Josh up and he molds to my hip. He smells sweetly soapy.

This time I'm the one who hesitates. "This one is for both of you," I tell them, and another bubble takes shape. Together we watch it float into the sun.

Selected Bibliography

Books

Bravo, E. *The Job/Family Challenge: A 9 to 5 Guide.* New York: John Wiley & Sons, 1995.

Brazelton, T. B. *Toddlers and Parents: A Declaration of Independence.* New York: Dell Publishing, 1989.

Brody, G. H. and Sigel, I. E. (eds.) *Methods of Family Research: Biographies of Research Projects.* Vol. 1, *Normal Families.* Hillsdale, NJ: Erlbaum, 1990; 189–90.

Brott, A. Ash, J. *The Expectant Father: Facts, Tips, and Advice for Dads-to-Be.* New York: Abbeville Press, 1995.

Dunn, J. *From One Child to Two: What to Expect, How to Cope, and How to Enjoy Your Growing Family.* New York: Fawcett Columbine, 1995.

Dunn, J. and Kendrick, C. *Siblings: Love, Envy and Understanding.* London: Grant McIntyre Ltd, 1982.

Eisenberg, A.; Murkoff, H. E.; and Hathaway, S. E. *What to Expect the First Year.* New York: Workman Publishing, 1989.

Eisenberg, A.; Murkoff, H. E.; and Hathaway, S. E. *What to Expect When You're Expecting.* New York: Workman Publishing, 1991.

Faber, A., and Mazlish, E. *Siblings Without Rivalry: How to*

Help Your Children Live Together So You Can Live Too.
New York: Avon Books, 1987.

Fields, D., and Fields, A. *Baby Bargains.* Boulder, CO:
Windsor Peak Press, 1995.

Huggins, K. and Ziedrich, L. *The Nursing Mother's Guide
to Weaning.* Boston: Havard Common Press, 1994.

Illingworth, R. S. *The Normal Child.* 9th edition. Edinburgh:
Churchill Livingstone, 1987.

Jonas, B., and Jonas, M. *The Book of Love Laughter & Ro-
mance.* San Francisco: Games Partnership Ltd., 1994.

La Leche League International. *The Womanly Art of Breast-
feeding.* New York: Plume, 1987.

Lansky, V. *Welcoming Your Second Baby.* Minnetonka, MN:
The Book Peddlers, 1995.

Merrell, S. S. *The Accidental Bond: The Power of Sibling Relationships.* New York: Times Books, 1995.

Placksin, S. *Mothering the New Mother: Your Postpartum Resource Companion.* New York: Newmarket Press, 1994.

Tamony, K. *Your Second Pregnancy: What to Expect This
Time.* Chicago: Chicago Review Press, 1995.

Weiss, J. S. *Your Second Child: A Guide for Parents.* New
York: Fireside, 1981.

Articles

Albers, L. L.; Schiff, M.; and Gorwoda, J. G. "The Length
of Active Labor in Normal Pregnancies." *Obstetrics &
Gynecology* 1996; 87: 3; 355–59.

Axinn, W. G.; Clarkberg, M. E.; and Thornton, A. "Family
Influences on Family Size Preferences." *Demography*
1994; 31: 1; 65–79.

Beck, M. and Quade, V. "Baby Blues: The Sequel." *News-
week,* July 3, 1989; 62.

Catiglia, P. T. "Sibling Rivalry." *Journal of Pediatric Health
Care* 1989; 3: 52–54.

Clode, T. M. "The Second Time Around." *Baby Talk*, September 1996; 48–50.

Duncan, O. D.; Freedman, R.; Coble, J. M.; and Slesinger, D. "Marital Fertility and Family Size of Orientation." *Demography* 1965; 2: 508.

Eggebeen, D. J. "Changes in Sibling Configuations for American Preschool Children." *Social Biology* 1992; 39: 27–44.

Gottlieb, L. N., and Mendelson, M. J. "Parental Support and Firstborn Girl's Adaptation to the Birth of a Sibling." *Journal of Applied Developmental Psychology* 1990; 11; 29–48.

Kalish, N. "Safe and Sound." *Sesame Street Parents*, April 1997; 48.

Legg, C.; Sherich, Z.; and Wadland, W. "Reaction of Preschool Children to the Birth of a Sibling." *Child Psychiatry & Human Development* 1974; 5; 3–39.

Leung, A. K. D., and Robson, W. L. M. "Sibling Rivalry." *Clinical Pediatrics* 1991; 30: 5; 314–17.

Levine, B. "Why Isn't My Second Child Walking Yet?" *Sesame Street Parents*, April 1997; 45–46.

Moscone, S. R., and Moore, M. J. "Breastfeeding During Pregnancy." *Journal of Human Lactation*, 1993; 9; 83–88.

Rooks, J. P.; Weatherby, N. L.; Ernst, E. K. M.; Stapleton, S.; Rosen, D.; and Rosenfield, A. "Outcomes of Care in Birth Centers: The National Birth Center Study." *New England Journal of Medicine* 1989; 321: 1804–11.

Ruben, D. "Planning to Adopt? How to Tell Your Children." *Parenting*, August 1997; 191–92.

Spock, B. "Sibling Wars: How to Keep the Peace—and Your Sanity." *Parenting*, August 1997; 129–34.

Teti, D. M.; Sakin, J. W.; Kucera, E.; and Corns, K. M. "And Baby Makes Four: Predictors of Attachment Security among Preschool-Age Firstborns during the Transition to Siblinghood." *Child Development* 1996; 67: 579–96.

Trause, M. A., et al. "A Birth in the Hospital: The Effect on the Sibling." *Birth & Family Journal* 1978; 5; 207–10.

Wagner, M. E.; Schubert, H. I.; and Schubert, D. S. P. "Sibling Constellation Effects on Psychosocial Development, Creativity and Health." *Advances in Child Development & Behavior* 1979; 14; 57–148.

HILORY WAGNER is the author of *The New Parents Sourcebook*. She also writes for *Parenting, Parents, Child,* and *Baby Talk* magazines. She lives in New England with her husband and two children.